YES

IS THE ANSWER.

WHAT IS THE QUESTION?

Cameron Mitchell's "Yes is the Answer. What is the Question?" is a candid, revealing and highly instructive chronicling of his inspiring journey from a troubled youth, through the Culinary Institute of America---and on to extraordinary success in the restaurant industry. The CIA Family is extremely proud of Cameron and I recommend this book to aspiring entrepreneurs and seasoned business veterans alike.

– DR. TIM RYAN - President, The Culinary Institute of America

"Yes is the Answer. What is the Question?" is a must-read for anyone who wants to learn the secrets of one of the legends of America's amazing restaurant industry.   From his start as a 16-year-old dishwasher to one of the most respected and admired leaders in hospitality, this book chronicles the spectacular results that come when an authentic leader and an organization put their people first.

– DAWN SWEENEY - President & CEO,
National Restaurant Association

Cameron Mitchell's deep commitment to his team's personal well-being and professional development permeates his narrative of his company's founding, setbacks, and remarkable success. His book is an important and instructive read for anyone dedicated to building a positive culture while growing a profitable business.

– LENA G. GOLDBERG, Senior Lecturer of Business
Administration, Harvard Business School

Honest and unique ... A penetrating insight into the mind of a successful founder ... wonderful example of performance and purpose.

– LESLIE H. WEXNER, Chairman and CEO, L Brands, Inc.

YES
IS THE ANSWER.

WHAT IS THE QUESTION?

CAMERON MITCHELL

IDEAPRESS
PUBLISHING

IDEAPRESS
PUBLISHING

COPYRIGHT © 2018 Cameron Mitchell
All rights reserved.

Published in the United States by Ideapress Publishing.
IDEAPRESS PUBLISHING | WWW.IDEAPRESSPUBLISHING.COM
All trademarks are the property of their respective companies.

Typesetting: Donald Ruppert

Cover Design: John Newmann

Cataloging-in-Publication Data is on file with the Library of Congress.

ISBN-10: 1-940858-71-2

ISBN-13: 978-1-940858-71-5

PROUDLY PRINTED IN THE UNITED STATES OF AMERICA
BY SELBY MARKETING ASSOCIATES

SPECIAL SALES

Ideapress Books are available at a special discount for bulk purchases for sales promotions and premiums, or for use in corporate training programs. Special editions, including personalized covers, a custom foreword, corporate imprints and bonus content are also available.

*To all the Associates of
Cameron Mitchell Restaurants.*

I am your Raving Fan.

CONTENTS

PROLOGUE

In April 2018, Harvard Business School held a course on the restaurant industry—the first in the school's ninety-year history. I was honored to serve as a speaker at one of the lectures, but more importantly, I was happy to see the nation's most elite business school focus attention on our industry. Restaurants are the second-largest private employer in the United States, overlooked for far too long as a major influence on countless aspects of the American economy.

2018 also marks the twenty-fifth anniversary of Cameron Mitchell Restaurants. Today, our sixty food service operations, including restaurants, The Budd Dairy Food Hall, and Cameron Mitchell Premier Events, span from coast to coast, employ almost 5,000 people, and generate over $300 million in annual sales. I have written this book because for many years, wherever I've gone, whether visiting our restaurants or speaking at conferences, I receive the same questions again and again: 1. How did you build such a successful business? and 2. Where do you find so many great people?

The answer to the first question is simple: Our incredible company culture, which is embedded in everything we do, is the most important factor in our company's success. The answer to the second question is essentially the same. We hire the same people everybody else does, but our culture nurtures and promotes their greatness.

I have written this book to tell the story of our company and the story of our culture, which began before we opened a single restaurant, back when I was a young man with a dream, a pen, and a yellow pad of paper. I wrote down five questions and answers that articulated who we would be, why we would exist, and what we would believe and do as a restaurant company. These questions and answers became the pillars of our company culture along with a philosophy built on eight core values, which have guided us for twenty-five years. I am confident that they will continue to do so for the next twenty-five years and beyond.

One of the most distinguishing features of our culture is that we place our associates first. While most other restaurants say that their number one mission is to take care of their guests, we make our associates our top priority. We have learned that when our associates are respected and cared for, they give our guests great service and genuine hospitality. As a result, our guests become raving fans and return again and again.

This book includes not only our successes, but also moments of failure and mistakes. I have written it for our industry, other service businesses, and anyone who is curious about our company. Most of all, I have written it for our people—those who work for Cameron Mitchell Restaurants now and those who will join us in the years to come.

In these pages, I also recount my personal history, including my difficult childhood, my time as a teenage runaway and drug dealer, my search for purpose, my life-changing journey through the Culinary Institute of America, and my great fortune to have a wonderful family. I candidly share both highs and rock-bottom lows in the hope that I can inspire others.

Yes Is the Answer. What Is the Question? is the title of this book because it has been a cornerstone of how we've done business since our earliest days. We see ourselves as great people who deliver genuine hospitality; therefore, we treat guests in our restaurants the same way we would treat guests in our own homes. It is natural to us that when a guest asks us for something, we say yes. We go out of our way to care.

Our *yes* attitude extends far beyond guest service. When an associate requests time off to care for family, or when a local charity asks for a donation, or when a purveyor or other company we do business with seeks a favor, the answer is yes. *Yes* is not a tactic we use to manipulate people into working harder in a scheme of greater profit. *Yes* is the answer because it is who we are, and the right thing to do. Our success is a byproduct of that philosophy.

A chocolate milkshake emerged as the symbol of our *yes is the answer* philosophy based upon an experience I had one rainy Saturday afternoon in 2002 when my family went out to a local restaurant for a late lunch. I was with my wife, Molly, her parents, and my two sons, then ages four and two. Molly didn't want to go to the restaurant because she thought it was not a kid-friendly place, but I persuaded her because I wanted to try a particular dish there. Finally, she agreed.

Not long after the six of us settled down at our table, a server appeared and began to take our orders. She went around the table, and got to me.

"I'd like a grilled cheese for my son," I said.

This seemed simple enough, but I really stumped her.

"I'm sorry, sir. We don't do grilled cheese sandwiches."

I paused for a moment and looked at the menu again.

"Okay, then, can I have a club sandwich? And please hold the turkey, the ham, the bacon, the middle slice of bread, the lettuce, tomato, and mayo. Then take what's left over and sauté it on both sides?" (Yes, I will admit that I was inspired by the famous Jack Nicholson scene in the film *Five Easy Pieces*. But if the server recognized the reference, she wasn't charmed.) Begrudgingly, she said yes.

I asked her to add a chocolate milkshake, too.

She looked uncomfortable.

"Sir, I'm afraid we can't do that, either. All we have is a large Häagen-Dazs milkshake on the menu, and it would be way too much for a young child."

"I understand. But would you please ask your manager?"

I watched our server walk over to her manager and explain. From across the room, I could see the manager shake her head while her lips formed the word *no*. The server returned to the table.

"Sorry, sir. We just can't do it."

"Would you please send your manager over to our table?"

By this time, my wife was kicking me under the table and asking me not to make a scene.

"I'm not going to make a scene," I reassured her. "I just really want to know."

Then the manager arrived. She reiterated that they couldn't make a small milkshake because they pre-portioned the ice cream, and if they used less than one serving, it would throw off their inventory. I had spent my life in restaurants, and knew they didn't pre-portion ice cream, but I forged on with a smile.

"Well, how about a chocolate milk instead?" I asked.

She was visibly relieved. "Of course, I can get you a chocolate milk."

She thought she was delivering hospitality at that point and turned away to get the chocolate milk.

"Excuse me," I said. "Before you go, I have a question…." I pointed to two items on the menu, a warm carrot cake and a hot brownie with the option of à la mode for $2.95.

"What does à la mode mean?" I asked.

By now, Molly was looking away, trying not to associate herself with the persistent guy sitting at her table.

"Oh," the manager replied, "that is a scoop of ice cream added to the dessert."

I said, "Really? Oh, cool. Can I have an order of à la mode to go with my chocolate milk? And would you mind whipping it all up in a blender?"

"Okay, sir," she said with an admonishing tone. "But that will be expensive."

"I'm a big boy," I said. "I can handle it."

She left the table, and my wife fumed. "I told you they don't take care of kids here. I can't believe their attitude. We're never coming here again."

We had the rest of the meal, and it was fine.

A couple of weeks later, I was the keynote speaker for our local business magazine, which was hosting an event celebrating the fifty fastest-growing companies in Columbus, Ohio. There I was onstage, proud as a peacock in front of 500 people, sharing the milkshake story and proclaiming that such a thing would never have happened at a Cameron Mitchell restaurant, where we provide genuine hospitality—a.k.a. great service. My speech was well-received.

A week later, a woman came up to me and said, "My husband heard you speak at the Hyatt, and he thought you were great."

I smiled and thanked her.

"He especially loved the milkshake story. But you know, afterwards, he went into one of your Fish Market restaurants and ordered a milkshake. The bartender said no, he was sorry, but they didn't make chocolate milkshakes."

I couldn't believe what I'd just heard. She might as well have punched me in the gut.

The next Monday morning, I arrived at our senior executive meeting, still reeling from the experience. I recounted the story and asked our team, "What do we need to do to reinforce for our people what we've been teaching all these years: *The answer is yes. What is the question?* What do we need to do to drive it home? Clearly, we have not made the impact we'd hoped."

That day, we brainstormed and decided that a chocolate milkshake would become the symbol of our culture. We would use the milkshake story and the beverage itself again and again to emphasize that the answer is always yes, and that we are great people delivering genuine hospitality. Today, each person who starts working at Cameron Mitchell Restaurants receives a chocolate milkshake and goes through a four-hour orientation to our culture and values. Milkshakes appear at regional meetings, special events, and other important moments. Managers celebrate associates who win our weekly Milkshake Award, for going above and beyond the call of duty, with a milkshake toast. We even created a company icon with a picture of "Flo the Waitress," who shares a beaming smile and extends a tray with a chocolate milkshake on it. Today, we make thousands of milkshakes a year, and celebrate our important events with this symbolic drink and toast—sometimes in humorous and surprising ways—to reinforce to our people: *The answer is yes. What is the question?*

YES IS A STATE OF BEING

Yes is more than a word. It is a powerful concept and state of being, not only in customer service, but also in life. For this reason, the title has personal meaning to me because I deeply believe in caring for people and giving back as much as possible. I have tried to lead my life by pushing out into the world all the good I can. As I see it, the more we give, the more we get back.

I believe in karma. Certainly, I came from very little, and have been fortunate to have received so much. I am indebted to society for the opportunities I've received. I am indebted to thousands of people who have helped me along the way, including the investors and mentors who believed in me. I am indebted to the people of our company, who always have and always will come first. None of our success would have been possible without the love and support of my wife, Molly, and none of it would have mattered without my children and the many friends and family members who have supported me unconditionally through the years.

At Cameron Mitchell Restaurants, we all have different job descriptions, whether server, marketing manager, or CEO. But all five thousand of us share the same role: to make raving fans of the five groups of people with whom we do business. These include our fellow associates, our guests, our purveyors, our partners, and the communities we serve. I hope that you, the reader, will become a raving fan—not only of our restaurants, but also of this book and what I share in these pages about building a great culture.

I welcome your feedback.

Cameron Mitchell
cameron@cameronmitchell.com

1

LOST AND FOUND IN COLUMBUS, OHIO

–

1972–1984

"What time is Dad coming home?" My mother and I were driving home after school in her sky-blue Oldsmobile. I was nine years old, riding in the passenger seat.

No response, so I asked again.

"What time is Dad coming home?"

"He's not," she answered, looking ahead at the road, expressionless. I watched her profile, waiting for an explanation.

"We're separating," she said.

When I asked her what that meant, she could tell me little more. I think she didn't understand it herself.

The car was silent for the rest of the drive home, and I looked out the window, watching the streets going by—stunned by the shock of it, unable to feel or cry. There had been no preparation, no discussion. No goodbye. When I got home, his belongings were gone. I didn't understand.

Until my father left, I thought my life was fairly normal. Sure, my parents had their fights, and sometimes my mother stayed in her room for days on end, and I could hear her crying. My oldest brother and my father fought bitterly at times. I remember being in bed and hearing the cops at the door. But I didn't know whether all of this was normal or not. I was a young child, and this was the life I knew. To a certain extent, it was a typical life. My father was an insurance agent, and though money was short, we lived in a middle-class house and always seemed to get by. I played Pee Wee football and Little League baseball, like other kids. My brothers were smart and did well in school. And there were some good times, like the year my parents saved up enough money in a shoebox so we could go to Florida on spring break.

Before things fell apart: my parents, my brothers Brian and Geoff, and me as a baby, 1963.

My father's departure marked the end of all that. Soon, things began unraveling. Every other weekend, I started to see my father for visits at his house, which I found terribly boring. The arrangement didn't last long, and by the time I was in middle school, he was out of my life.

My mother seemed to suffer from depression and mental illness, though I wasn't nearly old enough to understand these things. My dad never talked to my brothers or me about it, or tried to explain. Years later, when my two older brothers became medical doctors, they agreed that she probably had bipolar and narcissistic disorders. She was a very difficult woman with many highs and lows who had a hard time keeping it together, but I had no doubt that she loved me, and I loved her.

My father wasn't a bad guy. He just wasn't very smart or lucky. He had harebrained schemes that didn't pan out, like the time my mom inherited some money and wanted to use it to buy stock in The Limited and Wendy's—two young companies founded in Columbus that ended up doing spectacularly well. My father disagreed and talked her into investing in a dumpy apartment complex in Marion, Ohio. They never saw that money again.

After my father left her, my mother got a job as an administrative assistant, and we moved to an even smaller house in the have-not side of town. One thing I never understood was why my wealthy uncle didn't help her out. His wife's father had founded a large grocery-store chain, and whenever we visited, I was awestruck by their huge home and pool, their housekeeper, and especially the two refrigerators in their kitchen. I wondered why my uncle couldn't see that his sister, a single mother with three sons, was struggling. Perhaps he could see but was unable to help for whatever reason. Once a year, they took us out to their prim and proper country club, an experience I found unbearable because I knew we didn't fit in.

GOING ON THE RUN

I made it through grade school, but as soon as I arrived in junior high, things began to go wrong. On my first day of seventh grade, an eighth-grader named Harley Rouda came up to me and asked if I wanted to smoke a cigarette. Harley would later turn out okay, and eventually even run for U.S. Congress, but at the time, he was a lot bigger than I was—intimidating, and tough. Though I had never smoked before, I nonchalantly said, "Sure," wanting to go along. From then on, I started hanging out with the hoods and troubled kids who were smoking cigarettes in the bathroom, getting caught, and getting suspended. By the eighth grade, I was into drinking, smoking marijuana, and taking pills. By the ninth grade, it was more of the same—just progressively worse.

Upper Arlington High School was a tenth- to twelfth-grade high school. The summer before I was to begin, my mother suddenly decided that we were moving to Naples, Florida, for a fresh start. Evidently, my uncle had finally offered her assistance with a $50,000 loan. Her plan was to get a real estate license and work in the booming housing market down there. We packed up and went, and I attended high school there for four weeks. Then, just as suddenly as we had packed up and left Columbus, she decided that we were leaving Naples and going home. Fortunately, our house had not sold.

She'd probably gotten scared that she wasn't going to make it and wouldn't be able to pay her brother back. In Columbus, I showed up for tenth grade during the second month of school, which made my life seem even stranger. On top of it all, my hormones had kicked in while I'd been away, and suddenly I was growing tall and thin and becoming an angry young man. Also, I was starting to attract attention from girls.

When I got into high school, I started dealing drugs. At one point, I told my mother, "By the way, I'm going to Florida next week." I was only fifteen years old, but I made it clear that there was nothing she could do to stop me. I'd raised $7,000 from the kids at school and had a grand plan with my dealer to buy a hundred-pound bale of weed in Florida for $70 a pound and resell it for $350 a pound. I was entrepreneurial even then, and my love of numbers was obvious as I calculated my potential profit. But I was not yet sharp enough to avoid getting ripped off. The whole plan was a scam, and I came back to Ohio without the money or the marijuana. I had to start my business all over again with small amounts until I made enough money to pay everyone back. Once I got that done, that was the end of my drug-dealing days.

Word got out of what I was up to. The parents in the community understandably tried to keep their kids away from me. They especially didn't want their daughters anywhere near this pariah. I was awful. I smoked and drank at home. I didn't do homework. I came and went as I pleased, and let my mother know that she had no control over me. She made empty threats and cried and carried on, and I didn't listen to a word she said. She was not equipped to handle a kid like me. I can't imagine how much I made her suffer.

One morning in early April of my sophomore year, we were getting ready for the day when she said, "I've got an appointment for you at Franklin County Children's Services." Something in her tone was more serious than in the past. I looked at her face and saw exhaustion. Here was a woman whose husband had left her, whose fresh start in Florida had failed, whose two older sons had grown and gone, and whose remaining child was running wild. She was at the end of her rope and meant business.

Franklin County Children's Services was the agency that dealt with problem kids, and I feared she'd have me declared incorrigible. If that happened, I might have to go to court, be removed from home and put in a juvenile facility or group home. I didn't know exactly what could happen, but the prospect of that meeting scared me enough that I went on the run. After she left for work that morning, I threw my clothes into a bag and left a note on the kitchen table: *I'm not going to Children's Services. I'm leaving. I'll let you know where I wind up.* Then I called a friend to give me a ride to the Ohio State University campus, where I knew a guy who had a place. I shared his one-bedroom apartment along with several other runaways. It was only a couple of miles from home, so to throw people off my trail, I got a ride to Cincinnati, where I mailed a postcard to my mother. It said, *I'm okay. Don't worry. I'll be in touch.*

My newfound family and I stole cars, broke into people's homes, or found odd jobs that lasted a day or two. We did what we had to do in order to pay the rent, eat, and survive. Sometimes, I went days with little or no food, saving my change for a box of Kraft macaroni and cheese—made with water because I couldn't afford butter or milk. Yet all the while, whether I was fighting on the street or stealing something, I knew, deep down, that what I was doing was wrong and wasn't the real me. I knew I was going against my nature, which was fundamentally good-hearted. I just didn't know how to reclaim myself. Maybe that's why in June, on my sixteenth birthday, I set out to kill myself by overdosing on Quaaludes. I had a bag of them, and took a few. I was going to take the rest, but a friend grabbed the bag out of my hand and stopped me. The truth was that I really didn't want to go through with it, but I was so desperate and depressed.

The summer went on in the same awful way until September. The night before my junior year was to begin, I was sitting in that apartment when I felt an overwhelming force, something I still cannot explain, lift me up off the couch and send me over to the phone, where I called my mother. I'd had no intention of doing so. Perhaps it was some kind of divine intervention. Suddenly, there was my mother's voice on the other end of the line.

"Mom, I'm coming home."

An hour later, I was at her front door, barefoot, wearing only a t-shirt and jeans, with no other possessions. She threw her arms around me and cried. That night, we talked about everything and made a pact never to let anything like that happen again. We hugged it out and forgave one another.

The next morning, I arrived at school for the first day of junior year wearing the only thing I could find in my closet: a pair of suit pants and a button-down shirt.

The following week, I looked at the life I'd returned to and took stock of my situation. I could see the truth with full clarity. I was on my own. My mom couldn't give me lunch money, and my dad no longer paid child support—I hadn't seen him in years. I told myself that no one was going to take care of me except me.

From then on, I did not expect or seek help from teachers or other adults. Yes, I spent time in the principal's office, being disciplined for being late or cutting class. He was kind and saw the good in me, but he was not my mentor. The only other adult figure who came close was the high-school debate coach. During my junior year, he went out of his way to befriend me, and encouraged me to come by after classes and chat. I enjoyed debate competitions, and was thinking of becoming a lawyer.

He knew I had no father and was short on money, so he gave me work on weekends, helping him with projects at his house, after which he and his wife fed me dinner and talked about life. I accepted his friendship and appreciated it. He was also a well-respected pillar of the community.

Little did I know that he was engaging in classic grooming behavior. The next year, his intentions became clear when we were on a school trip. He conveniently discovered a mistake with hotel reservations; he was one room short. All the other kids were paired up, and somehow, I was the odd man out. "You can stay with me," he said, and I thought nothing of it. That night, I woke up and found him on top of me. I told him no and pushed him off, and he finally relented. I left the room and never spoke to him again. The experience did not shatter me, but I was hurt and angry. Years later, at my fifth high school reunion, I found out that he was a pedophile who'd preyed on other students, too. I reflected on why kids do not report these things, surprised that even I—a tough, streetwise kid—had never filed a complaint or told anyone, simply because he was the teacher and had the position of authority. After that reunion, I wanted to file charges, but it was too late; I learned that he'd died by then.

MY FIRST RESTAURANT JOB

Being on my own meant that I had to find work, and I was finished with my drug-dealing career, so I got my first job as a dishwasher at a steakhouse called Cork & Cleaver, making $2.65 an hour. I had no idea at the time what this would mean for the rest of my life. All junior year, I worked there for pocket money while struggling to get through school. I bussed tables and did prep work, such as cutting onions. I immediately took to the environment at Cork & Cleaver. I enjoyed seeing the guests coming and going, and I thought the staff was cool. Though the work was hard, I found the people energizing and fun. On my first night, my coworkers handed me a huge box of toilet paper and told me to take it to Tim the bartender and tell him that he needed to put it in the basement. The bar and restaurant were crowded, and Tim was busy making drinks. I squeezed through the crowd, carrying my big box of toilet paper. *Excuse me. Excuse me.* Finally I made it.

"Tim, I was told to find you. This box needs to be put in the basement."

He looked at me and shook his head.

"There is no basement."

We had many such laughs. I loved the camaraderie. Unfortunately, the school part of my life was not nearly as fun. I was social, and my classmates saw me as the guy who was always ready to have a good time, but inside, I never felt as if I fit in. Upper Arlington was an affluent town with clear lines between the haves and the have-nots. I was clearly in the latter group. I looked at kids who had intact families and vacations every year, and I coveted what they had. When it came to academics, I had the *can-do* but not the *will-do*. My grades were a mess.

At the end of my junior year, it came time for elections for senior class president, and I had the crazy idea to run. I gave a killer speech, promising all kinds of ridiculous concessions from the administration, but most of all, I distinguished myself by promising that if I were elected, I would arrange for a senior class trip to Florida. The gym thundered with applause. To my shock, I won.

The next year, I delivered as promised and rented two RVs and roped in two twenty-one-year-old co-workers at Cork & Cleaver to be our chaperones, which basically meant they would buy us beer and drive the RVs to Sarasota. We had fifteen kids in each RV. In retrospect, I am surprised that thirty sets of parents allowed their kids to do this. We parked at our hotel and used the RVs for transportation. Everyone had a great time. Meanwhile, I marked up the cost of the trip to cover my time and effort. The profit was enough to buy my first car. I guess you could say it was my second entrepreneurial endeavor.

Despite being the class president and the senior class trip hero, I didn't get to deliver a speech or walk with the Class of 1981 on graduation day because I missed passing sophomore English by less than one point on my third try. Even though I got an A on the final, the teacher failed me because of attendance.

Logically, I knew it wasn't the end of the world—but I couldn't help feeling humiliation and regret. I decided that from then on, no matter what, I would always do what it took to cross the finish line. After summer school, I finally graduated, ranking 592 out of 597 in my class. My grade-point average was 1.05.

AN EPIPHANY ABOUT THE FUTURE

After high school, most of my classmates went off to college, and the fall was lonely and quiet. Though I always expected I would get a degree someday, I didn't see the point of going to college if I had no idea what I wanted to do. Without a clue, I felt left behind and miserable. No longer a boy and not yet a man, I was still living in my mom's house, working at a low-level restaurant job for beer money—going nowhere. Even though I believed I could succeed, I couldn't figure out how to change things. I had been fired from every other job I ever had—delivering newspapers and mowing lawns.

When the Columbus restaurant chain Max & Erma's opened a fourth restaurant in December 1981, they hired me as a fry cook at $4.50 an hour. I was still immature and lazy, taking shortcuts whenever I could, hoping no one would notice. This went on for quite a while, until my boss suspended me for three days for being late one too many times and put me on thirty days of probation after my suspension. That hit hard. I had barely survived hitting the streets, barely graduated from high school, and now was barely holding onto a job. Would I ever get myself sorted out? Even with these regrets, I arrived at work late again during my probationary period. My boss could have fired me on the spot, but instead he forgave me and said, "Get out on the floor and get to work." Perhaps he had some faith in me; maybe he was just desperate because we were so busy.

Either way, I went to work that Friday worried that my life would never turn around. I was working a double shift, and happy hour had started at the bar. It was a very busy night, even for a Friday. The evening rush was building, and there was pandemonium in the kitchen as the managers barked out orders. Meanwhile, the bar was vibrating with people and the dining room was filling rapidly. I looked out at the kitchen. The clamor of human voices filled the restaurant, and the energy was frenetic. I loved everything about it.

Then something happened that I can describe only as an epiphany. Suddenly, I froze in place for about thirty seconds, and time seemed to stand still. With clarity, I could see my path. *I love this business. This is what I'm going to do. I'm going to be in this business the rest of my life.*

That night, I went home and feverishly wrote out my goals:

Go to the Culinary Institute of America, learn about food, and get a culinary degree. (I had heard the CIA was the Harvard of culinary schools.)

- By age 23—executive chef.
- By age 24—general manager.
- By age 26—regional restaurant manager.

- By age 30—VP of operations for a restaurant company.
- By 35—president of a restaurant company. (I wasn't thinking of owning a company at the time.)

It was 1:00 a.m., and my mother was asleep, but I knocked on her door anyway and burst in with the paper in my hand.

"Mom, I finally know what I'm going to do with my life."

She sat up groggily and switched on the light, listening while I shared my plans. When I finished, she was fully awake and ecstatic, which was not surprising, considering all I'd put her through. "You're going to be so good at it," she said. "I can't wait to see your success." I hugged her.

The next day, I showed up at work a changed person. The day before, I'd been the laziest guy in the kitchen, working for the man to earn beer money. In less than twenty-four hours, I'd changed direction 180 degrees to become the hardest-working guy in the kitchen. I had goals now, and for the first time in my life, I could envision a future for myself. This made all the difference.

FIRST STOP—HYDE PARK, NEW YORK

I applied to the Culinary Institute of America, located in Hyde Park, NY, which sent me a disappointing response. *You have good experience, but your grades are insufficient,* the letter said. My heart began to sink, but I kept reading and found hope. They encouraged me to go to my local community college and take a math course and an English course. If I did well and reapplied, they would look favorably upon my application.

I took those courses at Columbus State Community College the following spring. (I didn't know how fortunate and blessed I would be to stay involved with both institutions of higher education throughout my life.) When I put my mind to it, I was a good student. I got As in both courses and sent my grades to the CIA, which quickly replied with the good news: I was accepted to start the following January.

FORGIVENESS

I wish I could have said goodbye to my father and told him my plans. I imagine he would have been proud, but it was not to be. I'd reached out to him more than a year earlier. By then, he had remarried and faded away from my life. I'd gone years without seeing him, with one exception in my senior year when I was driving in the pouring rain. I'd accidentally cut someone off. No harm was done, but the guy in the other car honked and gave me the finger. That guy turned out to be my dad. He had no idea it was me.

During the time after high school when I was trying to figure out my direction, I started thinking about him, and realized that I didn't want to go my whole life without forgiving my father or having any connection with him. I was nineteen years old, and wanted to forgive him and get to know him. I called him up and asked if I could come by his office and say hello. He said, "Sure," and we set a date. When I arrived, I was struck by the odd familiarity. He was still working in the same rented space he'd been in when I was a young boy and used to visit on Saturdays. Everything looked the same. We chatted a little, and I began to drop by every few weeks to say a quick hello. My father had never been a touchy-feely kind of guy, but he seemed happy to see me.

I'd arrived at a difficult time in his life. His wife had been struggling with breast cancer for a long time, and she had just been diagnosed as terminal. Not long after my first visit, she declined quickly and went into the hospital. I visited a couple of times and found them in terrible condition. She was incoherent, and my father was distraught. She died soon after.

I began spending more time with my dad. About a month after his wife's death, he said he wanted to help me buy a car. We met on a Saturday morning and went out to dealerships to have a look. He took me clothes shopping, too, and we had lunch together. It was the first time in ten years that I'd spent a day with my father, and it was a great day. By the afternoon, we had a car picked out. I left to take care of the paperwork for the loan, and we made a plan to meet up that evening at a restaurant bar he frequented. When I walked in the door, I saw him talking with people, and he was smiling and animated. He seemed happy. We sat down at a table and ordered drinks. I handed him the loan papers, which he looked over and signed, and we agreed that the next day, I would get the car, then bring it over to his place to show him.

But that's not what happened. That night, around one in the morning, the phone rang. It was my brother calling to give my mother some news. She woke me to say that my father had died, apparently from an aneurysm.

My heart was filled with sadness for all that never was. I never got to know my father. He never got to see me go to culinary school, or start my business, or meet my wife and children. But I feel lucky that I had forgiven him and that when we'd said goodbye for the last time, we were on the road to getting to know each other. For many years, I wondered how I would have felt if I had never reached out. Surely, I would have regretted it my whole life. What we had in the final moments of his life wasn't nearly enough, but it was something, and at least I could feel some peace in the fact that I'd tried.

2

SHARPENING MY SKILLS
AT THE CIA

–

1985-1992

My departure for culinary school came in January 1985 and collided with a historic meteorological event. I was all set to make the nine-hour drive to the CIA, but an arctic freeze seized the eastern half of the United States for several days, killing people, crops, and livestock. Interstate 80 was shut down by snow and blizzard conditions, and at the last minute, I had to buy a plane ticket and fly instead. The morning I left Columbus, the weather was minus eighteen degrees, with wind chill—a jarring parting. I had sold all my furniture and said goodbye to a three-bedroom apartment, my beautiful girlfriend, and all my buddies during the worst winter freeze I could remember—all for an unknown future.

I had been to New York City only once before and didn't know my way around, but somehow, I found the bus from JFK to Grand Central Station. All my packing was intended to fill the trunk and back seat of my car. The last-minute change to air travel left me loaded with so many bags that I couldn't walk more than thirty yards at a time. A stranger saw me struggling and offered to help get me into the station and down to my train track. I thought he might be setting me up, but desperation made me say yes. He turned out to be fine, and I gave him a small tip, happy to get on my train.

The ride from New York City to Poughkeepsie, the closest stop to Hyde Park, took an hour and a half, and was freezing cold. It was zero degrees outside, and the wind blew up through the couplers and windows, rattling me the whole way. I dug out more layers of clothing from my bags, but nothing helped. When I got off at the Poughkeepsie stop, it was dark, and everything was covered in snow. After hauling my belongings from one side of the terminal to the other, one bag at a time over snow-covered steps, I took a cab to a crummy roadside hotel with drafty, chilly rooms. Even inside, it didn't get above fifty degrees the entire night. I slept in my clothes, shivering.

It was in this frozen and shell-shocked state that I presented myself at the steps of the CIA the next morning: twenty-one years old, no money to my name, and wondering if I would ever feel warm again. Staffers helped me get my bags up to a dorm room the size of a closet, where I set myself up on the top bunk. Naturally, I began thinking of my girlfriend, the master bedroom of the warm apartment I'd left behind, and my kitchen-manager job at Max and Erma's. I asked myself, *Am I really doing the right thing?* Over the next few days, I reassured myself that I was not going to fail. By the end of the first week, I knew I was in the right place. It felt like home.

I fell in love with the CIA, and though I couldn't have known it then, my connection to the place would last a lifetime. Years later, I would join the CIA's board of trustees and become the first alumni board chair as well as the youngest chair in CIA history. For now, though, I was just another young student at the beginning of a journey.

The Culinary Institute of America, America's greatest culinary school and my
alma mater, which I have been honored to support my entire life.

The CIA is located in a former Jesuit seminary on the banks of
the Hudson River. To my young eyes, Roth Hall, the main building
at the center of campus, exuded power with its huge brick edifice,
sweeping steps, and iconic columns. The school had been founded
in Connecticut in 1946 as a training ground for GIs returning from
war. By the time I arrived, it was the undisputed Harvard of culinary
schools, with an enrollment of about 2,500.

Everything moved at a brisk pace. Within twenty-four hours, I
was wearing chef's whites and a toque on my head, learning how to
chop onions and celery properly. The school's block system rotated
us quickly through three-week sessions, which immersed us in basic
techniques of making stocks and mother sauces, braising, poaching,
roasting, frying, preparing charcuterie and fish, and baking breads
and pastries. To this day, the memory of buttery croissants coming
out of the oven is indelible to me and most other CIA students. I
thought I'd gain weight there, but instead, I lost it from working so

hard. We got up early and worked late. We learned in class, staffed the on-campus restaurant kitchens, and honed our skills by doing. The rapid-fire instruction ensured that we not only received a thorough foundation in high-quality food, but also learned systems for kitchen brigade, restaurant service, kitchen cost management, and so much more. Standards for quality were relentlessly high, and the CIA discipline of doing things the right way turned into a way of being and living for the rest of my life.

WORKING THE LINE AND SCRAPING BY

I will never forget one French cooking class when the chef, an intimidating but soft-spoken man, pointed out the window at the gardens on campus. It was a summer day, and everything was green and lush.

"See this picture out the window here? If I gave you each a watercolor set and had you paint this scene, I would get twenty very different pictures." Then he turned from the window and said, "The talent lies within."

He was talking about how twenty people can work from the same recipe and yield twenty different products. Cooking is not objective. It always reflects the character of the individual who does it—all the small choices he or she makes from start to finish, the attention to detail, the personal finesse, and the commitment to doing things correctly.

In addition to teaching thousands of students, the CIA drew a constant barrage of tourists. They came to eat in the campus restaurants and roam the halls each day, peering in on us as if we were in a fish tank. I didn't mind this theatrical aspect; in fact, I thought it was cool. The observing eyes of certain great chefs were another matter, because some scared the crap out of you. German and French culinary culture dominated the CIA in those days, and the foreign chefs were like gods from Olympus.

Our purpose was to learn all the classic culinary techniques and recipes of Northern Europe, from *escargots* and *soufflés* to *Wiener schnitzel*. More important, we learned the traditions of Auguste Escoffier, who codified the French culinary canon and created the infamous militaristic hierarchy of the professional kitchen. As students, we were in a form of servitude, and they expected us to go obediently down the river, learning their program, their way. This was the CIA tradition, and it graduated some of the top culinarians of the world. The two years I spent there were kind of like drinking out of a fire hose. I loved it and thrived on it. I don't think I've learned at a pace that fast ever since. The CIA got into my cells, and I would remain connected for the rest of my life.

As I saw it, there were three kinds of CIA students: those who were gunning to be chefs, those who wanted to be in the restaurant business, and those who were lost and had gone to culinary school because they weren't scholarly and didn't fit in anywhere else. I was in the second category. I loved the line in the kitchen, working the sauté or the broiler station, or expediting the process. I worked hard, but in my heart, I knew I was not a great chef and never aimed to be. It wasn't in my DNA. My purpose at the CIA was to get a foundation in food and cooking so I could succeed in the restaurant business.

Money was a constant stress. My mother didn't have anything to give me toward tuition, and I spent my two years there struggling and scraping from a patchwork of funds. My middle brother helped me out, I got a Pell Grant, the school gave me financial aid, I took out loans, and I worked. But each semester, I went through an incredible rigmarole with the financial aid office, never sure I'd have enough.

After they were convinced that I'd exhausted every other resource, they always gave me aid.

A couple of weeks into my first semester, I went home and re-trieved my little beat-up BMW so I could work at restaurants in New York City on Saturdays and Sundays. During my two years at the CIA, I held jobs at Tavern on the Green, the Waldorf Astoria, and the Grand Hyatt at Grand Central. At each of these places, I was the ex-tra pair of hands in the kitchen: *Hey, cut this, prep that, peel these bags of onions*. But they paid well, and I got New York kitchen experience, which was very important to me. With that said, the drive from the CIA to Midtown took an hour and forty-five minutes, and because I had nowhere to stay in the city, I made four drives each weekend. After a week of grueling classes, I would get myself to Midtown on Saturday morning, put in a twelve-hour day, then drive back to the CIA. On Sunday morning, I did it again to reach the kitchen at eight o'clock, not to return until six or seven o'clock at night. During one period, I went almost a hundred days without a day off.

Tavern on the Green had an old-school New York noir feel to the kitchen—the kind of place where the cooks used to drink beers while they worked. Outside behind the kitchen door, you might see fifty to a hundred rats. I'd go out for a smoke with the other cooks, and those rats would look at me like, *Hey, what are you doing, man?* They weren't the slightest bit nervous. This was New York City.

There were many tough scrapes, and times when I had to impro-vise—for example, the Sunday I came out of brunch service at the Grand Hyatt and my beat-up BMW wouldn't start. I had six bucks and a Gulf Oil gas card in my wallet. That was it: no AAA, and no one to call. The car was parked near the corner of Lexington Avenue and 42nd Street. I took a few steps toward the intersection and noticed that Lexington graded slightly downhill. The car was a stick shift, so

I pushed it out, turned onto that street, jumped in, and popped the clutch. Thank God, the engine caught, and I drove home.

Sometimes, when I drove the West Side Highway, I passed an island off to the side where stolen and abandoned cars were propped up on cinder blocks and stripped down to the frame. In a few desperate moments, I fantasized about running out of gas there, letting the car get stripped, and putting in a claim to the insurance company so I could pay my tuition. I never did, because I knew it would be wrong, probably wouldn't work, and would leave me no way to get to my job. Thankfully, in a couple of tight spots, my brother again came through with money to help me finish school.

Because of my work schedule, socializing was out of the question Friday through Sunday nights. That left me Monday through Thursday. I set up a system in which I carved out two nights a week to enjoy life at the CIA with my friends. We played racquetball and went to Pizza Bob's, where they served draft beers for a quarter and cheap pizza. We had a good time for about five bucks each. But partying took a back seat to my education. The other two weeknights, I forced myself to stay in and study or read industry journals and business books as an extension of my education. I knew why I was there.

At the time, the CIA offered only associate's degrees. The bachelor's degree came in 1993. As my second year wound down, I began to consider altering my original plan and continuing my education so that I could earn a business degree in hospitality management. Around that time, the school hired buses and drove students to the Westchester Marriott to hear a talk from Marriott's worldwide vice president of food and beverage operations. After he finished, I shot up to talk to him, ready to impress, and told him I was thinking of going to Cornell's School of Hotel Administration when I graduated from the CIA.

Before I could get too far in my spiel, he said, "You have received the best education here. Get out and get going. You don't need to attend college anywhere else."

I took his advice to heart and stuck to my original plan.

About six months before graduation, I began looking across the country for jobs in hopes of lining one up the month before I finished. I knew I would be working for the rest of my life, and I wanted to relax and enjoy my remaining time at the CIA without a lot of responsibility.

Whether it's luck or the seeds we plant earlier in life, I can't say, but about a month before graduation, I was in my French cooking class when a familiar face showed up at the door. It was Jeff Hollenbeck, the old food and beverage director from Max & Erma's. He was in the area on business and stopped to see the school and seek me out.

"Hey, I am taking this job as the corporate chef for the new 55 Restaurant Group in Columbus. Want to be my sous chef when you graduate?"

I wasn't sure. Columbus was home, and I always knew I'd go back, but this would be sooner than planned. I'd been interviewing and hoping to get an offer in Kansas City at one of the Gilbert/Robinson restaurants, such as Plaza III The Steakhouse. On the other hand, I liked Hollenbeck, and didn't want to say no.

"Yes, I'm interested," I said. "Can I come to Columbus and learn more?"

Back in Columbus, Engine House No. 5 was one of the best restaurants in the city: a fantastic upscale seafood spot located in a nineteenth-century firehouse owned by Chuck Muer Restaurants, which was based in Detroit. Muer owned many restaurants in the 1970s and 1980s before he died at sea during a Florida storm in 1993. Four Columbus guys—a group of land developers, architects, and wealthy businesspeople—used to have lunch regularly at Engine House No. 5. While they were soaking in the food and atmosphere, they hatched plans of starting their own restaurant on the first floor of a building they owned.

Of course, they knew nothing about restaurants, but when the foursome came for lunch, they often found Richard Stopper in charge, and got to know and like him. Richard was a regional manager for the Muer Corporation. Clearly, he did a great job, so they tried to hire him to launch their company. Because Richard had a son and was tired of traveling around the country for his job, he liked the idea of being closer to home—plus, he could get in on the ground floor of something new, he agreed to come on board. Within a year, Fifty-Five On the Boulevard, a white-tablecloth restaurant named after its address at 55 Nationwide Boulevard, opened to accolades. The restaurant quickly became a top-ten eatery in the city.

When I flew into Columbus, I went straight to the restaurant to meet Richard. We sat at a table and talked, hitting it off right from the start. Richard told me that the businessmen backing the 55 Restaurant Group wanted to build more restaurants, and that this was an up-and-coming company with lots of opportunity. The second restaurant would be called Fifty-Five at Crosswoods, on the north end of Columbus—another white-tablecloth restaurant much like the original Fifty-Five. He needed a sous chef.

"Hey, where are you going after this meeting?" he asked.

"Back to the CIA."

"Well, if you have time, let me take you to the new restaurant first."

We got into Richard's car and drove over to the space. It was being renovated, so he took me inside the office trailer and showed me the blueprints. We walked the construction site and talked some more. He and I spent hours together that day. When the phone rang, he told the caller that he had a guy named Mitchell sitting in his office who was going to be his new sous chef. "You're going to hear a lot more about this kid," I remember him saying.

The next day, I called him and formally accepted the job. Before we hung up, Richard told me he'd be working on the new menu, and if I had any ideas, I should let him know. I went back to the CIA and burned the midnight oil for a week, then sent Richard a package with several dozen menu items to consider. I still had about a month before I graduated, so I had achieved my job goal with time left to relax and enjoy my final weeks at school.

Celebrating graduation from the CIA in 1986, with my girlfriend at the time Bev, sister-in-law Peggy, brothers Geoff and Brian, and my mom.

FROM SOUS CHEF TO PUNK

After I graduated in October 1986, I packed up the car and drove back to Columbus. The next Monday morning, I reported to Richard Stopper and Jeff Hollenbeck. I was twenty-three years old and ready.

Two months later, we opened Fifty-Five at Crosswoods, a 250-seat restaurant. It was successful and busy from the start, and I loved it. As Jeff's sous chef, I was second-in-command in the kitchen, running the prep list, jumping into stations where I was needed, and doing some purchasing. It was a great learning experience. Jeff was a fellow CIA graduate and had a terrific background as a director of food and beverage at Max and Erma's restaurants. He mentored me, as well. Richard was sharp and well trained by the great Chuck Muer, and he passed that training on to me. (I used to say I was a second-generation Chuck Muer guy.)

As a sous chef, I was driven, working twelve- to fourteen-hour days without batting an eye, then getting up and doing it all over again. Six months after I started, the executive chef at the original Fifty-five started to have problems on the job, and Richard had to let him go. He gave me the job. Almost a year after that, the general manager left, and I was promoted again.

The new position was great, and I met my goal of becoming a general manager by the time I was twenty-four. However, I still had a lot to learn because in reality, I knew nothing about leading people. As executive chef, I'd been intense in the kitchen, prone to yelling and acting aggressively with my colleagues if I thought things were going wrong. More than once, Richard and Jeff had to remind me to calm down. When I became general manager, I knew little about the front of the house because I'd never been a server or bartender before. Richard gave me some training, but I was a micromanager and made classic micromanager mistakes, following around the old-time professional servers and looking over their shoulders. I'm sure they looked at one another and asked, "Who is this punk?"

One day, Richard called me into his office and shut the door.

"I just finished a meeting with eight servers who threatened to quit if you don't leave. I don't want you or them to leave, so I convinced them you would change. And that means I need you to change immediately."

I was completely blown away. I'd had no idea. After I recovered from the shock, I went to the local bookstore, grabbed a few leadership books, and began to study. I realized that my style had been all wrong. I'd gotten the idea that it was all on me, that the restaurant's success was a direct result of how much and how hard I could work, like an inverted triangle with the point on my shoulders. I changed immediately. Instead of worrying so much about how I did my job, I switched my energy to helping other people do their jobs.

This became a defining moment in my young career. I learned that you can't lead with integrity unless you put your people first.

The problem was that my reputation preceded me, and when I was subsequently appointed as general manager at the Crosswoods 55, the staff expected me to kick in the door and say, "A new sheriff's in town." When I walked in the door for the first time, I had the sense they were waiting for me with bows and arrows drawn.

I had a one-on-one with each associate for five or ten minutes, acknowledging my reputation, but asking each one to keep an open mind and give me a chance, because I'd changed my ways. I promised they wouldn't regret it. The associates responded at an incredibly high level, and the restaurant became a happier work environment.

TIME TO FLY

By 1990, we had opened two more restaurants for the guys who owned 55 Restaurant Group, and I started to blossom. I was promoted to operations manager. Now, four of us were running this group of four restaurants: Richard at the helm, Jeff in the heart of the house, me in the front of the house, and our chief financial officer. By early 1992, we were up to six restaurants. It was tremendously educational to be on the ground floor of this startup. Our offices were right next to the owners' offices. This gave me the opportunity to sit in on meetings and observe how expansion worked—from how they raised money to how they negotiated leases and made floor plans. Such firsthand knowledge would be incredibly useful to me later. If I'd taken a job in that Kansas City restaurant corporation, I never would have had the chance to learn so much.

The downside was that the owners may have been decent guys individually, but as a group, they didn't seem to give a rat's ass about us. Sometimes they'd take up residence at a table, and I dreaded the inevitable moment when one would holler at me across the dining room to get him another drink. They had no knowledge of the restaurant business, and we had built a small empire for them, but they didn't seem to respect us for the work we did. This was in the era before the food revolution, when chefs and restaurateurs were not part of a highly respected profession in American culture. There was no doubt they saw the managers of their six restaurants as hired help.

Things started to take a turn. My goal was to become the president of a restaurant company by age thirty-five. Now I was almost twenty-nine, with no upward mobility in sight. Richard was president, and he wasn't giving up the top spot. There were no more rungs on the ladder, not to mention that my relationship with Jeff was declining because our personalities started clashing. One day, I told Richard my goal was to make $100,000 a year.

"Well, you might want to look for another job if that's what you want to make."

My salary was about $80,000 at the time, so this was not motivating to hear. I was exasperated, and sensed the end was near. But where was I going?

Soon afterward, I went to a local restaurant on a Friday night to meet a friend. I was waiting at the bar, feeling discouraged as I thought about my future. The dinner rush was over, but the place was still packed. The owner was a chef, and I looked up and saw him out in the dining room, wearing his chef's coat and talking to guests. They were smiling, and he was laughing. Everyone else on the floor looked on with appreciation. Here was a man who had created something that was his. Everyone seemed to want what he had to give.

It was another of the moments in my life when time stood still, and suddenly, I could see with great clarity the direction I should take. I've described these moments as epiphanies, but they did not strike by lightning. The vision came out of an intense combination of frustration and seeking. This time I heard a voice in my head say, *I'm going to start my own restaurant company.* I'd never thought of having my own company before; my plans had always focused on being president of someone else's restaurant company. I'd never dreamed about having Cameron Mitchell Restaurants, but it was suddenly so obvious as the only way I could get where I wanted to be. My next thought: *If I am going to be president of a restaurant company at thirty-five, I'd better get moving.* I envisioned working at the 55 Restaurant Group another six months to a year while I saved some money and made a plan. Then I'd strike out.

Unfortunately, in my enthusiasm, I told some friends that I was going to open my own restaurant, and word got back to Richard.

"Where are you going to be a year from now?" he asked me a few weeks later. He and I were out driving together, with him at the wheel.

I evaded the question. "I'm not sure."

"Are you happy here?"

I looked out of the window and took a breath. I couldn't lie to him.

"I'm happy here, but I also want to grow more. I want more things for myself. I am trying to sort it all out."

Then we were silent.

A few days later, he asked me to meet him at the office on the following Saturday morning. As soon as I walked in the door and saw his face, I knew what was coming.

"This is going to be the best thing that ever happened to you," he began. He fired me, then said, "It's time for you to fly."

After six years at the 55 Restaurant Group, I walked out of that office for the last time.

3

ONE YELLOW PAD AND DOZENS OF PARTNERS

–

1992-1993

After leaving the 55 Restaurant Group, I felt like a son leaving home to go into the world alone. It was inevitable that I would leave—and though it had happened sooner than I'd expected, I couldn't be mad at Richard Stopper, because he had let me go in a caring way and taught me so much. With my severance check and a small IRA, I had less than ten grand to my name, so I had to figure out my next move quickly.

The Monday morning after I was fired, I woke up and sat down with a pen and a yellow legal pad, trying to think clearly about how to proceed. If my dream had been to start a restaurant, my first step would have been to head out the door and look at real estate, searching for the perfect location. But my plan was to start a restaurant company, which this was a very different undertaking. I turned inward and began asking myself questions about the big picture. What kind of company did I want to build, and what would be its identity and purpose? What kind of principles would lead to success? What would be its culture?

During the next few weeks, I worked on, developed, and wrote out my ideal company culture and values. Then I set about building a restaurant company based upon that culture and those values, and I am still doing this, twenty-five years later. I reflected on my twelve-plus years in the restaurant business and all the good and the bad I'd witnessed, trying to create a vision that would retain all the positive experiences and discard all the negative. What was great about working in a big restaurant company, and what was awful? What was great about working in a mom-and-pop place, and what usually went wrong?

I recalled the way one of the owners of the 55 Restaurant Group had shouted at me from across the room to get them a drink. And I remembered a server at Crosswoods, a guy who was spectacular at his job, but arrogant to his coworkers. Why had I tolerated that? I thought about my own mistakes, such as yelling in the kitchen when I was a young chef, and how much better everything began to operate once I changed my behavior from micromanaging to supporting people. One thing I had learned without a doubt was that when the staff was happy, restaurants functioned well, guests were happier, and the quality of everything went up. Could I create a company in which associates genuinely liked to be at work, and were valued as the most important part of the business?

THE CUSTOMER COMES SECOND

During this period of searching and planning, I read business books for days on end. I was especially influenced by *The Customer Comes Second and Other Secrets of Exceptional Service,* which had just been published. The author, Hal Rosenbluth, described how he had joined his family's travel business right out of college and discovered a miserably unhappy environment. Most of the employees didn't like one another, and as far as he could tell, they weren't particularly nice people, either. Rosenbluth decided he wanted to build a company of friends, and this meant hiring nice people and creating an environment that bred friendship and mutual support. As his thinking evolved, he set out to create a new culture in which, above all, employees were valued, empowered, and therefore motivated to care for their clients. He succeeded, and the company's success rocketed into the billions.

As soon as I began reading, I knew I'd found a vision that articulated exactly what I believed. This kind of enlightened management was sorely missing in the restaurant world. I got to wondering why restaurants so often treated their employees as disposable commodities. Why did the industry typically have such a high turnover rate for staff? Certainly, most restaurants tell you that treating guests with hospitality is their number-one reason for success. But if the chefs, bartenders, and servers who interact with guests are treated poorly and have one foot out the door, how well could they ever treat those guests?

I decided that the restaurant company I was going to build would put associates (I did not want to label them employees) first, not the guests. This went against conventional wisdom, which said that guests always came first. It's not that I didn't believe service was a priority. Nothing could have been further from the truth. Hospitality still runs to the deepest depths of my heart. I don't care if someone is black or white, male or female, eight or eighty; I love to take care of people. But to achieve such hospitality, you must take care of your people first.

Management generally does not have a direct relationship with restaurant guests, but the staff does—all associates have contact, direct or indirect, with guests. Suddenly, I could perceive the triangular relationship at the heart of my model. The company takes care of its associates, the associates take care of the guests, and the guests take care of the company, because they genuinely want to return.

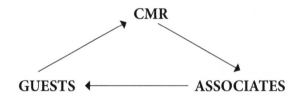

At this point, I was just a guy sitting in his living room, trying to formulate what I believed into a clear mission and culture that would become the framework for the company I wanted to build. My approach took the form of a dialogue: I wrote down five simple questions and answers on the yellow pad. These five questions and their answers became the pillars of our company. I believe that any company or organization must be able to answer these five questions with authority and conviction:

OUR PILLARS: THE FIVE QUESTIONS

Who are we? Great people delivering genuine hospitality.

How do we define this? Simply put, everybody has great people in their lives. We all have a sense of what that means, and can relate to the idea of great people. *Delivery* means someone has received something. *Genuine* means from the heart. *Hospitality* means treating guests as we would treat people in our own home.

What do we want to be? An extraordinary restaurant company.

By simple definition, *extraordinary* is the opposite of *ordinary*. There are hundreds of things we do every day that are the opposite of ordinary. We will do anything not to be an ordinary restaurant company.

We are always aspiring to be an extraordinary restaurant company.

Why are we in business? *To continue to thrive, driven by our cultural and fiscal responsibilities.*

Our job number one is to maintain our cultural foundation. We want to operate a restaurant company with the kinds of values that will keep it around for fifty, seventy-five, even a hundred years—long after I am in the big restaurant in the sky. To do this, we are guided by the knowledge that our decisions and actions are to be based 51 percent on our culture and 49 percent on profit. We want to make a profit, and a damn good profit, but we will never put profit on higher ground than our values. If that means we leave a dollar on the table in order to avoid sacrificing our culture, that's what we'll do.

What is your role? *To make raving fans of the five groups of people with whom we do business: our fellow associates, our guests, our purveyors, our partners, and the communities in which we do business.*

We have almost five thousand associates with different job descriptions, but we all have the same role: to make raving fans of the five groups of people with whom we do business. I agree wholeheartedly with Ken Blanchard's view of raving fans, and the definition of that phrase is common sense. It requires that whatever we can do to make raving fans of these five groups of people, we will do it. If it means a server needs the night off at the last minute, they get it. If it means making a cup of hot chocolate for the FedEx driver on a cold winter's day, that's what we'll do.

What is our goal? *To be better today than we were yesterday, and better tomorrow than we are today.*

We can't take this goal to heart without working at getting better every day, pushing to raise our game, and refusing to accept the status quo as good enough. Anyone we encounter could debate us for hours about how successful we are, but we probably can all agree that we are, at least, a *somewhat* successful restaurant company. With that said, here is our insurance policy: by being better today than we were yesterday, and better tomorrow than we are today. By virtue of this alone, we will create a culture of growth, and we will be an increasingly successful company every day.

We know these five pillars, we teach them, and they become the screen by which we measure everything. If we encounter an issue in our business that doesn't have anything to do with the five questions, we disregard it and move on.

After the questions were written, I knew I needed more. I needed to answer *how*. How would we go about delivering genuine hospitality? How would we become an extraordinary restaurant company? How would we thrive and make raving fans of these five groups of people? How would we achieve our goal of being better today than we were yesterday, and better tomorrow than we are today?

Over the course of three weeks, as I sat in my shorts and t-shirt, surrounded by dog-eared books and articles ripped from magazines, I wrestled with these questions. I blocked out everything else. Slowly but surely, the words began to come together.

To answer these questions, I wrote down a company philosophy based upon eight core values.

OUR PHILOSOPHY: EIGHT CORE VALUES

1. We Believe Our Associates Come First

Our people are the foundation of this organization. When our company puts its people first, the results are spectacular. The tools we utilize and the theories by which we operate all stem from this belief. Superior service comes from the heart, and cannot be faked. We realize the guests we serve will have a wonderful experience only when our associates are truly happy.

2. The Whole Is Greater Than the Sum of Its Parts

We never hold on higher ground the value of an individual over the value of the team. For the team to function at its greatest potential, all individuals who comprise the team must work in harmony to ensure this. It is important that no individual can disrupt the positive chemistry of the team.

3. Attitude, Attitude, Attitude

To preserve our great work environment, we hire only upbeat people from a variety of cultures and backgrounds. Positive attitude is a way of life; it is a conscious choice and the driving force behind exceptional service. Everyone is responsible for fostering an atmosphere that encourages positive attitudes.

4. Work Should Be Fun

We have an exciting work environment that is filled with laughter and smiles. Guaranteed fun = guaranteed success.

5. Quality Is Built in up Front and Permeates Everything We Do

We believe there is no room for mediocrity. If we are not better than the rest, we become a commodity chosen only for price. We measure our quality constantly. What we choose to do, we choose to do well. It is not the one corner cut, but the sum of all corners cut, that becomes the damage done. Our quality is 100 percent guaranteed. We do it right the first time.

6. We Foster Open and Honest Communication

Communication breaks down the barriers to success. We uphold an open-door policy. Feedback creates learning, understanding, and growth. The only bad idea is the one left uncommunicated. We communicate only through respect and eloquent language. When we are all informed, we can move forward together.

7. We Believe in the Creative Process

There is art in everything we do, and we promise to stop and take time to smell the roses. Art is important, because some of the most memorable aspects of service are creative ones. Pride should be taken in even the simplest tasks to be completed. Time, people, ideas, artistic beauty, and togetherness all define the creative process inherent to our success and organization.

8. We Are Committed to the Growth of All Our Associates, Our Company, and Our Community

We are committed to both company and personal growth. We believe that without the growth of our associates, we, too, would become stagnant. Everything changes around us, and we intend to change with it, not be left behind or forgotten. We are committed to the educational process. We believe that learning should last a lifetime, and the more our associates learn, the more we will know.

Our culture and values became our compass. If something did not fit within the framework of the five questions and eight core values, then the company wouldn't do it. Since the early days when I wrote them, the five questions and eight values have never failed us.

The final piece of our company culture and values is: *Yes is the answer. What is the question?*

What does this mean? It means that if we can do it, we will. Most people will say no if they can, because *no* requires taking no action. We say yes, we can do that—if possible. If that means we're showing you to a table, and you like another one, the answer is yes—we'll do our best to accommodate you. If you ask us to make something that's not on the menu, but we have the ingredients, it may take extra time—but we'll try our best to make it. We don't hire chefs who won't make changes to the menu because they have intellectual pride about the integrity of their dish. That's bull. If we don't serve root beer, and your kid is thirsty for root beer, your server will go across the street and buy one. Yes. We will donate a gift card to your school fundraiser. Yes. We will allow a server who is a single mom to start her shift later to accommodate her child-care needs. Yes. I could probably fill an entire book with examples of of our culture in action. Instead, the appendix of this book contains just a few of our favorite letters, notes and emails we've received over the years.

And just to be clear…does this mean you can bring a gun to work? No. Does this mean you can sexually harass your coworker? No. Does this mean you can smoke in the dining room? No. But saying yes is giving a damn for those five groups—our associates, guests, partners, purveyors and communities—and making the effort to live it.

THE BIRTH OF CAMERON'S AMERICAN BISTRO

With the company culture and values down on paper, I was ready to take the next step: a location. I didn't know exactly what I wanted, other than a space that was manageable in size and had a good location. What made a good location? I didn't have the experience to understand this fully, but right away, I found a space I liked in Worthington, a suburb of Columbus. It was a little meat shop that offered about thirty-five hundred square feet of restaurant space, on the end cap of a strip center in a great location, with easy access to the highways. When I met the real estate agent there, she tried to crank up the pressure. "Hey, well, listen, Cameron," she said. "I have three other people interested. If you are going to move, you better do it quickly, because this is going to go fast."

I was a very green entrepreneur and simply couldn't hurry. Plus, she intimidated me, so I put that space on the back burner and moved on to an interesting site—the Battleship Building, named for its riveted steel panels that evoke the hull of a battleship. It was located at 444 North Front Street, in the hub of an expanding downtown neighborhood near the convention center. I thought it seemed like a great space, so I struck a preliminary deal with the landlord. Now all I needed was to raise $600,000, and that meant writing a highly convincing business plan, and describing the restaurant concept, market, management team, and projected cash flow.

I didn't understand much about restaurant branding at that time, but I thought a contemporary American-style bistro would be easiest to sell, so that was the plan. The menu would offer elegant but unfussy American and European favorites, from steak frites and seared ahi tuna to innovative pasta dishes. I hired a design firm to create a preliminary design that conceptualized the floor plan and kitchen as well as the look and feel of the place, which was a classy bistro atmosphere balancing formality and warm hospitality.

With my business plan prepared, it was time to go out with my best foot forward, exuding confidence and promise to potential investors. The problem was that my meager savings were diminishing, and it would be many months before I could raise all that money, build the restaurant, open for business, and draw a paycheck. Starting a restaurant company was a full-time endeavor, and I desperately wanted to avoid getting a job on the side, which would have made me seem less serious. It was important to me to appear professional from the start.

I turned to my family. They did not have a lot of money, but combined, they gave me about $100,000 of the total. It was a start. I called my oldest brother first. By then, he was practicing medicine and living back in Columbus. I asked him to become my first investor with a $50,000 investment. I also explained that I was running low on cash and asked him to make me a $12,000 loan that would get me to my first paycheck. He was ten years older than me and had left for college when I was only nine years old—around the time my father had left. Maybe he knew that he'd never been a big part of my life, and this was a chance to do something for me. He said yes to both requests.

My middle brother also contributed. He had just graduated from medical school, and took a cash advance on a credit card to help. My mother had remarried by this time, so she and her new husband, Don Noe, a wonderful guy, put some money in, too. My mother wasn't always great with advice, but this time, she had wisdom to share. She quoted from *Dave's Way* by Ohio native son Dave Thomas, founder of the Wendy's restaurant chain: "Surround yourself with good people." I took it to heart immediately. Years later, Dave and I would meet and become friends.

A few people were willing to do *quid pro quo* agreements. Among them was my insurance guy, who was a great guest of mine at the 55 restaurants. I told him that if he invested, I would buy my insurance from him, and since he knew how I operated, he was willing to take a chance. But such deals were few and far between. I had to hit the pavement and raise the bulk of the money.

Fundraising was an excruciating process filled with rejection. During the years of running six restaurants for the 55 Group, I had met many people from all over Columbus. Drawing on these contacts, I put together a list of two hundred and fifty prospects. My approach was to get in front of as many of them as possible, share my business plan, and make my pitch. I described the values and culture I wanted to build in my company and offered partnership agreements, projecting a return of partners' investments within three to five years. One in ten people said yes, and the other nine said no, which to me meant, "I don't really believe in you." I certainly understood—I was young and untested. After each rejection, I had to get up and go back out again. It was brutal, but I did it.

After almost four grueling months, I got there. A total of twenty-five investors signed on for amounts between $10,000 and $50,000. It was a huge accomplishment, and I was desperate to move forward. I called the landlord to finalize the lease so design and construction could begin, but something strange happened. He didn't return my call. Radio silence. After several more unanswered calls, I asked my attorney what he thought.

"Something is wrong," he said. "I don't know what is wrong yet, but something is *definitely* wrong. We'll find out soon enough. You've got to wait it out. If I were you, I'd start thinking about Plan B."

I was devastated. After all those months of meetings to raise the $600,000, my lease was falling through, and there was nothing I could do about it. Meanwhile, it was the second half of December. The holidays were coming, and the world was shutting down to celebrate with family and friends. I tried to rally for Plan B, as my lawyer called it, and went out in the snow and rain to look at other properties, but there was nothing worth seeing. Adding insult to injury, I had to move into my mother's condo because I was running low on money, and I'd been so busy working that I had no girlfriend or prospects. I spent the holidays in a deep, dark hole—the most depressed I had been since I was a high school runaway.

Finally, in early January, the landlord called.

"I ran into some financial trouble," he explained. "The bank wants to repossess the building, and they do not want a restaurant at the bottom of this building. I apologize, but I am going to go bankrupt, and you need to go away. Cam, I am so sorry I couldn't do this deal with you."

Though I was deeply upset, this news delivered me from limbo. At least I knew the deal was absolutely off, and the ball was back in my court. That's when I remembered the meat-market space— the first place I'd seen with the agent who told me to hurry because she had so much interest. It turned out that the place was still available, and the landlord, an attorney named Don Feinstein, agreed to meet me.

We hit it off, and he said he'd give me a chance. We worked out a lease, and he didn't even make me sign personally for it. To this day, he likes to tell people that without him, Cameron Mitchell Restaurants wouldn't exist—and he's probably right. I will always have a special place in my heart for Don, who remains one of our most ardent supporters. I quickly redid my business plan for the new location and put together a new legal partnership offering. This time, I needed only $400,000 because the place was smaller, a restaurant of ninety-four seats. I hit the pavement once again and returned to my investors, giving them back their uncashed checks along with the new business plan. Some lost interest or faith, but by February 1993, I had raised $360,000. I was 90 percent of the way there.

That's when everything came to a crashing halt. The money dried up. I had turned over every stone I could think of, but I had no clue where to get the remaining $40,000. A do-or-die meeting was coming up on Friday morning with my two main partners: my construction manager and my attorney. If I couldn't move forward, they would pull out. All the money my brother had lent me was gone. My credit cards were maxed out, and I was down to my last seventy bucks, rolling change to buy groceries.

Before closing the first round of fundraising for Cameron's American Bistro in 1993, I was counting change to buy groceries.

I'd worn out my list of contacts long ago, but out of the blue, an idea came to me. One of my investors was a wealthy man named Bob Liebert, whose father had founded a major company in Columbus and sold it for a fortune. I didn't know Bob very well, but I suspected he might have more capacity, and I was desperate. I knew his assistant, Gail Zura, and called her, holding my breath while the phone rang.

"Hi, Gail. Any chance I could come in and see Bob?"

She put me on hold, and while I waited, I thought I heard my pulse getting louder. At last, she returned. "Bob will see you at 2:00 on Thursday afternoon." That was the day before my big meeting.

When Thursday arrived, Gail walked me to Bob's palatial office. He was welcoming and easy to talk to. I told him that I was stuck in my fundraising.

"How much do you need?"

At that moment, I had never lied in my business career, and I have never lied since. But I lied to Bob then.

"Thirty thousand," I said, shaving off ten grand. I was hoping he would agree to cover half that amount, which would get me to $375,000—enough I felt to buy more time at the meeting the next morning.

"Okay," he said, pulling out his checkbook. Just like that, he wrote me a personal check for the entire $30,000, saying, "Pay me back when you can." He added, "And use this to buy some more company stock for yourself. I wish you the best of luck."

That was when I knew I was going to make it. The next day, I showed up at the meeting with my construction manager and my attorney with $390,000 worth of checks in hand. My construction manager called two friends and said he wanted them each to put five grand into a restaurant company we were starting. "Cameron will come and pick the check up later. Is that okay?" It was, and I did.

By now, it was Friday afternoon, too late to go to the bank and cash the checks. However, I had a hell of a happy hour—and a hell of a weekend—because I knew I was going to get my company started. The following Monday morning, I went to the bank and opened a new account, Cameron's of Worthington Limited Partnership, and deposited the $400,000. It was March 1993. I wrote a check for $7,000 to reimburse myself for expenses, such as typing and producing all those business plans, and I lived on that for the next six months, until opening day.

THE BIRTH OF A COMPANY

With the funds raised, I could sign the lease. The next step was to go to the city council and get zoning approval. I needed to make my case that Cameron's American Bistro wouldn't create parking problems. At one point, I sat in my car for almost a week, from Monday to Friday between 11:30 a.m. and 2:00 p.m., recording the number of available parking spots every half hour to prove there would be sufficient parking capacity for our business. We were approved.

Two months before opening, I set up an office in the construction trailer and hired Stacey Connaughton, Julie DeLeo, Ed McArdle, and Mike Tibbetts. I'd worked with most of them at the 55 Restaurant Group, except for Stacey, whom I had known since junior high school (and who went on that senior class spring break trip!). Decades later, I would joke that I was employee Number 001, and she was employee Number 002. This was the opening team, and we overcame many hurdles to get to opening day.

On October 5, 1993, the last pieces of furniture were still being delivered in the afternoon, and nerves were high; but as the evening came, all the places were set, and the dining room looked beautiful. In the kitchen, the counters and stainless steel gleamed with newness. The chef and his staff were fully prepped, and the bar was stocked. Fourteen agonizing months without a paycheck since the day I had left the 55 Group, and finally, it was opening night. I stepped outside and looked up at the sign: *Cameron's American Bistro*. I wasn't nervous. I was excited.

My first restaurant is still thriving today: Cameron's American Bistro.

All week long, we were packed for dinner, and lunch was good, too. The Columbus press gave us great reviews. The second week, we were packed, and the third week, as well. That was when I knew we would be successful. I didn't need to see the P&L. In the first year, we brought in just under $2 million in sales, which was almost 50 percent more than my initial projection.

From day one, I knew that our success would depend upon making raving fans of the five groups of people with whom we did business: our fellow associates, our guests, our purveyors, our partners, and our community. We would have many challenges along the way, but I was determined to keep our values and our culture as the number-one goal. If it didn't fit within the framework of the five pillars or the eight core values of our company philosophy, then it wasn't worth doing.

Cameron's American Bistro was the birth of a company, and set a stepping stone to the future. Within a few weeks of opening, I was looking to find my next restaurant.

THE EARLY YEARS

–

1993-1998

When my first restaurant opened, I was thirty years old, single, and working so hard I hadn't been able to think about dating for a long time. About three months after we opened Cameron's American Bistro, an old acquaintance named Cathy walked into the restaurant with a girlfriend she introduced as Molly. It was a Saturday night, and we were packed to the gills, so it was all I could do to say hello, seat them, and get right back to work.

A little later, Cathy pushed through the crowd to chat with me. Soon, her mission became clear.

"Hey, Cameron. You dating anybody?"

When I said I'd been too busy opening the restaurant to find a date, she handed me a slip of paper with a phone number on it. "You should call my friend, Molly, and take her out."

When they said goodbye, Molly kept her head down and avoided eye contact. She was depressed over a breakup with a college boy-friend she had expected to marry, and mortified that Cathy had given out her number. This was all unbeknownst to me when I called Molly the following Monday and invited her out for a drink. She agreed, and we set a date for the following Thursday night. I later learned that she had almost called it off, but her mother pushed her to get out and move on with her life. When the night arrived, our two cars pulled up side by side at a local bar at the same moment.

"Molly?"

I had seen her at the restaurant a few days earlier, but it had been so busy, I wasn't sure I recognized her. Yes, she was Molly, and we walked into the bar together.

Shortly after we got settled, I asked her to tell me about herself. She told me she was from Cleveland, and was a sophomore English teacher. "I love reading," she said.

I couldn't help but laugh. She looked confused. "What was so funny?" She wanted to know, so I had to tell her the truth.

"I failed sophomore English three times. I read a book every couple of years, and I'm actually a couple of books behind."

Things could have gone one of two ways at that point, but we ended up talking until 1:30 a.m. and had a great time. We closed the bar.

The next day, I told a friend that I'd just met the person I was going to marry. Later, I found out that Molly had gone home that night and written the same thing in her journal. We were engaged seven months later.

It was a wonderful time of life, filled with energy and promise. I'd just opened a restaurant, I'd met a wonderful woman I was going to marry, and I was moving to open my second restaurant. I was ambitious and driven—a young man in a hurry, ready to take whatever risk was necessary to achieve my dream. What I needed most was capital, but first, I had to find a site.

The answer came in Bexley, Ohio. The owner of a French restaurant was ready to retire and was looking for someone to take over his lease. I liked the idea. For one thing, the space was an existing restaurant, so I wouldn't have to install a kitchen. Also, the location seemed like a natural. The first Cameron's was doing incredibly well in an affluent inner-ring suburb north of downtown Columbus. Bexley was an inner-ring suburb east of downtown Columbus, and because it was affluent, I assumed it would perform in the same way. Plus, many people in Bexley were regulars at the various 55 Group restaurants and knew me. I felt certain they'd be interested if I opened a place in their town.

A DEFINING MOMENT FOR OUR CULTURE

I wrote up a new business plan and launched another private placement offering, returning to my original partners, asking them to invest again, and reaching out to new prospects, as well. It wasn't much easier the second time, except that I had one successful restaurant as proof that I could do it. As with the first restaurant, my goal was a 30 percent annual return on the original investment, which was why I told my partners not to expect their investment back for three to five years. When I said I was going to open a second restaurant, most of them understood, but one partner was livid when he heard I was moving ahead before paying him back on the first. I tried to explain that I was building a company—not just one restaurant. If I waited until our partners got their investments back, it would take three to five years to open each restaurant. That was no way to build a company of any scale. After some deliberation and angst, I eventually bought his shares back. We needed only $350,000 this time, and we were able to raise almost all of it from existing investors.

With the lease signed and the funds raised, I was on target to open Cameron's of Bexley in the fall of 1994, one year after Cameron's of Worthington. The construction company had just gutted and broom swept the new space, and it was ready to build. Not long after that, I was standing there soaking in the moment when a local cop drove up and asked me what I was doing.

"I'm Cameron Mitchell. I'm opening my second restaurant here," I said proudly. We exchanged a few friendly words, but I glanced down the road and noticed a couple of women walking through the street. After a double take, I asked the officer, "Are those prostitutes?"

"Yeah, they are."

"Officer, is there a lot of crime around here?"

"Oh, yes. Someone just got killed across the way."

My stomach fell with a thud. Clearly, in my excitement to move forward, I hadn't done my homework, but it was too late to back out, and we had to move ahead.

Cameron's of Bexley opened to decent crowds, but nothing to write home about. The restaurant averaged only $20,000 to $30,000 a year in profit, and when equipment broke or unforeseen costs arose, that small profit got even smaller. Yes, the town was affluent, but it was surrounded by low-income neighborhoods where people didn't have a lot of money to eat out. I wound up closing it six years later.

Without another hit on my hands, there could be no illusions that I would open any more Cameron's American Bistros. I had no brand that I could replicate. Obviously, I needed a new concept.

I'd always idolized Richard Melman, a brilliant entrepreneur who had created dozens of diverse restaurant brands, from the Michelin-star-winning Everest in Chicago to casual chains such as Maggiano's Little Italy and the Bub City barbecue joint, plus dozens more.

The idea of creating a multi-concept restaurant company had always been in my mind, and now it really took hold.

Soon I had my eye on the Olentangy Inn, an old hotel along a less-traveled road between downtown Columbus and the Ohio State University campus. There had always been a 24-hour coffee shop in the front of the hotel, a cup-of-joe-and-a-piece-of-pie kind of place that was steeped in nostalgia. It seemed like a natural for an upscale diner. The trend for American comfort food was rising, and I was inspired by a trip I'd made to the Buckhead Diner in Atlanta, which was just killing it.

A developer had bought the hotel and was converting it into office space. I reached out to see if he would agree to a restaurant. I heard he was considering leasing the diner space, and I became obsessed with getting it. I knew it was a great location and began calling my lawyer every day to check on it. When he called to say we had the deal, I was ecstatic.

We signed the lease and set out to raise $600,000, with a plan to open in the fall of 1995. Fundraising wasn't easy, but it was becoming easier. I was starting to get traction with friends and investors who could see I had the talent, the drive, and the track record. We decided to call our place Cap City Fine Diner—a tribute to Columbus's role as our state capital. Then we set out to rehab the space, which was a run-down disaster filled with many decades' worth of books, records, and debris in the basement, and infested with cockroaches. I wondered what I'd gotten myself into.

In fact, we were just kids running restaurants back then, and there was so much we didn't know. What we did have going for us was a huge amount of energy and a commitment to high quality. Best of all, we had a great culture, which continued to drive all that we did.

From the beginning, we gave surveys to our staff every year to see if our culture, values, and mission were alive and well. These associate opinion surveys were simple, at first. With a staff of a few dozen people, I scored and compiled the data by hand. Years later, we'd use a computer and eventually produce a six-inch binder, twice a year, filled with data on associate performance and feedback.

Early in our second year, I faced a major challenge to our culture, one that threatened our most important value—that associates come first. It happened one night when I was at Cameron's of Bexley, and the general manager from our Worthington location called to tell me that the executive chef there had just called one of our servers horrible names, including the c-word.

I'd known this chef since we'd worked together at the 55 Group, and he was a talented and capable culinary guy. He'd been holding down the fort and running Cameron's of Worthington while I opened the new location in Bexley. I picked up the phone and called him.

"Is it true?" I asked. "Did you call her these names?" Yes. He told me it was true. "Well, I'll be right over there." He told me to put the pedal to the metal.

When I arrived at the restaurant, we escorted him off the premises within five minutes. I knew I had to fire him. If I didn't, I couldn't live with myself or our people, and I couldn't look at the woman he'd insulted. This is not to say that I deserve credit for doing the right thing, but I believe this was one of the defining moments of our company.

If I had caved and let him stay, it would have made a statement that this associate was more important than the others because he was a good chef, and that was good for business. If I had done that, I might as well have thrown our values out the window. If our culture had stated that the guests came first, then I probably would have reprimanded this chef, but kept him because he turned out excellent food, and that was in the guests' best interests.

As soon as I fired him, I was terrified of the repercussions. I had no replacement ready. I promoted two freshly-minted sous chefs to take over his role and work as co-executive chefs. It was not ideal, and I had to spend a lot of extra time coaching them, but we kept true to our culture. Later, I noticed that our people rallied behind me when I made such difficult decisions. Moments like these built the cultural foundations of our company and further strengthened us.

Occasionally, I've also had to "fire" guests for treating our associates poorly. Back in the old days of the restaurant business, when male guests came in, got drunk, and started touching or being rude to servers, it was standard operating procedure for management to ask the server to put up with it. "Come on. They are going to be gone in half an hour, and you'll never see them again. Just bring them a beer, and toughen up." Neither I nor our company ever operated that way because it was against our values. We put our associates first and would never ask them to put up with such behavior.

If a guest was abusive to our people, I always told the guest to leave and not come back. When someone was belligerent, I called the police. Clearly, one guest wasn't worth it. We would never sacrifice our values or culture for a random guest mistreating our associates.

Molly and I got married during the summer of 1995. We had a wonderful wedding and a honeymoon in Hawaii, but as soon as we returned, I threw myself right back into work. Cap City Fine Diner opened that fall. We created a fun retro design, and the menu offered classic diner favorites, usually with a twist: for example, mile-high meatloaf with shitake mushrooms, our signature dish, and blue cheese potato chips with Alfredo sauce.

Marrying Molly is the single greatest decision of my life. On our wedding day, 1995.

Cap City was extremely successful—a breakthrough. It was not uncommon to have a thousand people each day on the weekends. It remains our busiest restaurant ever.

Not long after we opened, I went to work one Sunday wearing a suit and tie. When the dishwasher called in sick, I had to fill in for him, so I called Molly and asked her to bring me work clothes. I met her in the parking lot and found her crying because she had not seen me much, and was worried that she'd married a workaholic. I believe in balance in life and never wanted to be one of those guys who succeeded in business at the cost of a miserable family. I hugged her and assured her it would get better.

That was my first lesson in balancing life and work. It was hard, because I was building a company, but I was overdrawn on my account with Molly. Immediately after returning from our honeymoon, I was absent for much of each week. I knew I had to make her a higher priority. I've worked hard to balance my life ever since, and it's always been a challenge because of my drive. If see a deficit, I spend more time with my family. The way I managed during those years and ever since was to allocate my attention and time in the same way I allocated funds in my accounts. When one got low, I shifted money over. This also worked with my relationships, and I spent more time with Molly.

With that said, Columbus was growing, and I was determined to grow along with it. A new convention center had just opened downtown, in the Short North District, and it would be the anchor for a major redevelopment of a fragile neighborhood. With the hordes of people coming in and out of that center all year and for decades to come, I knew it would be worth gold. When I saw a newspaper ad for a space right across the street, I jumped on it and met with the developer, Ron Pizzuti, who took a liking to me and gave me a lease. He also became one of my larger investors, and remains a great supporter of the company. He wanted me to do an Italian restaurant, so I agreed and again raised funds—another enormous undertaking. With Ron's help, we got it done.

BUILDING OUR AMAZING TEAM

We opened Martini Modern Italian in 1996. The design was sleek and sophisticated, and the food and bar were upscale. It was our fourth restaurant in three years, and because of the location and quality, it earned back the initial investment quickly, bringing in $80,000 a week. With our four restaurants, we had a $10 million-a-year business. I was giving all I had, but I was starting to run thin. I had never worked harder in my life. My core leadership team consisted of Stacey Connaughton, who handled accounting; Julie DeLeo, who managed human resources; and myself in operations. We had little to no business infrastructure or other management staff. It was time to develop a senior management team and create some needed structure and depth.

Around this time, I placed an ad for a director of operations in *Nation's Restaurant News* and received hundreds of resumes in the mail, plus one FedEx envelope containing a thoughtfully written letter from David Miller, who had spent a decade at Stouffer's Restaurant Company in Los Angeles. He wasn't job hunting at the time and didn't have a resume ready, but he'd been born and bred in Dayton, Ohio, and he and his wife had just decided they wanted to move their family back home. His letter stood out, so I picked up the phone, and we had a good chat for an hour. I told him I happened to have business in LA the next day. Would he be free to meet? He was, and we had an excellent meeting. I offered to come back the following day and have brunch with his wife so she could meet me. David was smart and experienced, and I had a gut feeling that he was the right person. In thirty days he had a starting role as general manager of Cap City Fine Diner, and not long after that, he became our first director of operations.

The next year, I searched for a chief financial officer. Again, I received many resumes, but when Diane Rimkus (now Diane Smullen) arrived in our office, she had a professional demeanor with an impressive background in restaurant finance. On top of that, her father was in the restaurant business, and she'd put herself through school working in restaurants. I thought she'd be great for the job, and I was right.

In those early days, I looked for strong experience and high-quality people, and of course, I always explained our company culture and values in the first interview. I made it clear that whoever joined the company would have to embrace our five cultural pillars and eight core values. Other than this, I had no understanding of who would succeed or fail—but, amazingly, many of these people are still with me and have made a huge impact on our success. Today, Diane is still our chief financial officer, and David is our president and chief operating officer. Stacey Connaughton, who began as our accounting manager and my assistant, has stayed by my side all twenty-five years, and is our vice president of corporate affairs. We all worked together to grow the company and develop as people.

TRANSPARENT, OPEN, HONEST COMMUNICATION

In 1997, we started to hold off-site retreats among the leadership team. They included Julie, Stacey, David, Diane, and me, plus our executive chefs and general managers. The first one was simple: We rented a van and went to Cincinnati to eat and drink and talk about the future. The next time, we rented a cabin in the wooded Hocking Hills of southern Ohio and brought more than twenty people, including general managers, executive chefs, and executive team members. We used the time together to solve problems, strengthen our culture, bond with one another, and have fun.

Transparent, open, and honest communication is a key value in our culture. I have always believed that everybody needs to know what is going on. The more we communicate with our people, the better off they are and the more connected they feel. That's why I used these retreats to tell our managers about our restaurant finances, investment partnership history, and fundraising efforts. We wanted our managers to understand the stakes when we pushed them for a good return. In most companies, corporate management keeps these numbers close to the vest, but I noticed how much they appreciated being in the know. We also used these offsite opportunities to discuss goal-setting, and I asked general managers to contribute benchmarks for the next year.

At one of these retreats, we came up with the idea of having ten restaurants by the end of 1999. It was a huge goal, but we decided to go for a full-on push because it would create a turning point for the company. And we went full speed ahead.

We had a significant time in 1997 when we opened two restaurants in the same year. For the first concept, we seized upon the growing trend of brew pubs in collaboration with a local brewery, the Columbus Brewing Company. In June, the restaurant opened to great reviews and overwhelming crowds. Then we opened a second Cap City Fine Diner, this one in the nearby town of Gahanna.

Now, we had six restaurants under our belt and a $15 million-a-year company. The workload was enormous. I'd raised capital six times by now, and it was always incredibly difficult. The last 10 or 20 percent was the hardest; sometimes it felt like scaling Mount Everest on my knees. The process was always frustrating and time-consuming, but it continued to become just a little easier each time.

Each new restaurant had its own books with its own set of investors, who were either limited partners or general partners (the latter guaranteed the bank debt and received a preferential return). With six restaurants, this meant juggling twelve sets of partners, keeping them informed, and making distributions according to their various investment levels and each restaurant's profit. It meant filing twelve different tax returns! We had created an accounting nightmare for ourselves.

This silo structure of ours served the purpose of survival. If one restaurant failed, it wouldn't take the others down. But now, with six restaurants in place and four more planned by the end of 1999, it was unsustainably complicated. We needed to create economies of scale, simplify our accounting, and form one company.

We hired Deloitte & Touche to do a valuation and roll-up all our restaurants into one entity. This would allow us greater efficiency and thus, greater cash flow, which would fuel further growth when needed—without requiring us to go out and raise more money every time we wanted to open a restaurant. We could grow on our combined internal cash flow.

Deloitte & Touche assessed the cash flow, assets, and liabilities for each of our six restaurants, and valued our entire company at $4 million. We decided to do one final capital raise that would infuse an additional $3.5 million into the company and allow us to open our next two restaurants: a steakhouse and a fish market, both new concepts that had been on my mind for a while.

The steakhouse idea had come to me while I was on a trip to Washington, D.C. and visited the wonderful Capital Grill there. I returned home thinking that Columbus also needed a grand steakhouse. A few days later, I walked out of a meeting downtown and noticed a *for lease* sign on a glorious old former bank space right across from the Statehouse. It had tall ceilings and stately architecture that was perfect for what I envisioned. The location on Third Street was on the main road into downtown Columbus. The area did not have a residential population; instead, it was filled with office workers who came in for the day and went home to the suburbs at night. I was getting smarter about site selection, and could see the enormous potential of the convention business, state workers, the state capitol building across the street, and weekend arts community. I wondered why no other restaurateurs saw the possibility. *Columbus Monthly* magazine certainly raised doubt when its annual list of *bests* and *worsts* honored Cameron Mitchell Restaurants with "best leap of faith" for our decision to locate a restaurant in this downtown neighborhood.

If a steakhouse seemed a natural for an Ohio city, a seafood restaurant did not. We were landlocked, and at the time, most Ohioans had not experienced fresh, well-prepared seafood. After all, the biggest body of water in our region was Buckeye Lake. I wanted to change that by building a fresh seafood restaurant that would bring in the top of the catch from coastal purveyors each day, with menus printed each morning to match because everything would be so fresh and varied. I had always loved seafood as a kid, and our family dinners at a restaurant called Seafood Bay. I wanted to introduce Midwesterners to a completely new style of eating fish. I hired an executive chef, Wayne Schick, who'd come from the Chuck Muer organization and had tremendous seafood experience. Then I found the perfect location on Olentangy River Road, just two doors down from Cap City Diner. Once again, I could see potential in this location, which was slightly off the beaten path. Coincidentally, this, too, was a vacant bank.

The steakhouse and fish market were far larger than anything we'd ever done before. Our budget for each restaurant was about $1.75 million—more than double what we'd ever spent before to open a restaurant. Stacey and I worked on proposals and business plans, then pulled together our dog-and-pony show to go out and raise money again. My first stop was our existing partners. This time, it was harder than ever because first, to pull all our restaurants into one entity, we needed all the partners to agree. It was a tough sell, because with the new infusion of cash and the combining of the restaurants, each partner would wind up owning a smaller piece of a bigger pie if they didn't reinvest. I had to go to all the partners and say, "Hey, you know that partnership you were in? Well, we're throwing it out and doing a new one, and it's fair, because Deloitte & Touche said it was. So if you want to keep the same percentage of ownership you already have, you're going to have to increase your investment." It took many conversations, and sometimes I had to meet with people again and again. This transition went on for months, but in the end, they all agreed to the transaction. The new entity, Cameron Mitchell Restaurants, LLC, was officially born in 1998.

MAKING RAVING FANS

With this transaction completed, we proceeded with the two new restaurants, which went over budget by $750,000. In the final hour, I was out of money and had to take out a bank loan to reach the finish line. Mitchell's Steakhouse finally opened in August 1998, and Columbus Fish Market followed one month later. The response was tremendous. Huge numbers of people began to arrive at our doors, and both restaurants quickly began to bring in over $100,000 a week each, an amount I'd never dreamed we'd see. By the end of 1998, we were able to pay off a significant chunk of the $750,000 loan.

It was a pivotal year. Sales at our eight restaurants reached about $25 million annually. We had our executive leaders in place, and we started to become well known in the city, receiving awards and great reviews. Our company maintained its strong culture and values.

The year of 1998 was pivotal for me personally, too. Molly and I had our first baby, our son Charlie, and my young family moved into our first house. I turned thirty-five. Though I was feeling good about life, there was no doubt that in the preceding five years, I'd expended an insane amount of energy, working six days a week and getting five or six hours of sleep at night. Often, I would come home from work to see Molly and Charlie for an hour, have dinner, and return to work until midnight. Those were days of incredible strength and determination, and the pace wasn't going to let up.

5

THE FIRST BIG EXPANSION

–

1999-2002

When 1999 dawned, we had eight restaurants in operation, and were well on the way toward our goal of having ten restaurants up and running by the year 2000. Our two big-bet restaurants—the Steakhouse and the Fish Market, which we'd opened the previous year in two former bank buildings—were continuing to go gangbusters. We had two more restaurants in the pipeline for the coming year. In June 1999, we opened a new concept that blended the two ideas: an elegant supper club that specialized in steak *and* seafood. It was designed with an imaginative nautical theme: a Jules Verne *20,000 Leagues Under the Sea* hardscape featuring cobalt blue tones, terrazzo floors, and murals of shells and mermaids. We called it Mitchell's Ocean Club, and planted it in a huge new shopping development in a northeast suburb of Columbus. We opened on the second floor, overlooking the first level. Our menu featured wild and naturally sourced seafood, prime chops, and steaks.

In the fall, we opened our second Columbus Fish Market and shortly thereafter, a second Mitchell's Steakhouse, in the Crosswoods development north of the city. As we grew, so did our staff. A talented chef named Brian Hinshaw wanted to come aboard. We didn't have an executive chef position open at the time, so he joined us as a sous chef at Mitchell's Ocean Club when it opened, then quickly rose to executive chef. I promoted Chuck Kline, a superstar executive chef who had started at our third restaurant in 1995, and Wayne Schick to corporate chef positions, overseeing our ten restaurants. It was enormously gratifying to see our culture at work: we were promoting associates from within, and they were experiencing huge success.

On New Year's Eve, we were brimming with optimism about the new millennium, and toasted our accomplishments of the prior years. We'd grown to eleven restaurants and seven separate concepts in less than a decade. Our company was flying, and people in Columbus were paying attention.

I loved the momentum, and wanted more. Our team and I decided to expand much more rapidly, and hatched a plan to build eight new restaurants in 2000 and 2001. The additions would be tough enough, but to make things crazier, only three would be in Columbus. The other five would be in Pittsburgh, Pennsylvania; Louisville, Kentucky; and Newport, Kentucky. Never before had we built a restaurant out of town—a big step for any company.

Compounding our risk, we did not research and select these cities. Instead we followed Columbus-area developers who were building new projects there and offered us opportunities. We weren't exactly strategic. We opened a Fish Market and a Cap City Diner next to each other in a new Pittsburgh development; ditto a Fish Market and our Martini Modern Italian in another lifestyle shopping center development in Louisville, Kentucky. We didn't think about how and whether they would complement one another. In addition, the developments were all new and unproven. If the shopping centers turned out poorly, we'd just doubled our losses.

RECKLESSLY SKIING DOWNHILL

At the beginning, we were euphoric, seeing this phase as the first step to going national. But some immaturity was at work, and some greed, too. If we could build ten restaurants, why not build one hundred? I didn't have a board of directors to slow down my entrepreneurial overdrive, and though I relied on our executive team and peer mentors to give me feedback, we all were young. We did not yet have the wisdom gained from experience. It was as though I kept skiing straight downhill, recklessly fast and over all kinds of terrain. Our team had no choice but to try and keep up with me.

Pittsburgh was our first venture out of Ohio, and it was the worst. Two of our executive leaders, David Miller and Wayne Schick, went there to open a Cap City Diner and a Mitchell's Fish Market—renamed for export from our Columbus Fish Market. We'd scheduled them to open in July 2000, within two weeks of each other. For thirteen weeks, David and Wayne drove from Columbus to Pittsburgh every Monday, then back home Saturday night. They had young kids, so the workload and being away so much was very stressful on them and their families. It also took a toll on their sleep. Just before the opening, Wayne fell and broke his foot, no doubt from exhaustion. When they found themselves in Pittsburgh for Halloween, they were pissed off at me. I tried to make it up to them, and chartered a plane at four in the afternoon so they could see their kids dressed up for trick-or-treating and spend the evening at home with their families.

Of course, many people on our staff were frustrated with me for working them so hard. I understood why, and I tried to lighten up when I could. It was my flaw, at the time, to be consumed with our company's growth, and I failed to grasp that our people's mental capital was precious and needed care like any other asset.

Amid all these stresses, there was joy. My second son, Ross, was born in October 2000. My family was growing alongside our company.

By the end of 2000, we'd opened three of our eight new restaurants—two in Pittsburgh and another Martini, this one on the north side of Columbus. As 2001 started, we had five new restaurants scheduled to come within a year. We had to undertake yet another round of fundraising from our investors, essentially doubling their investment again as the company was nearly doubling in size.

By the summer of 2001, we opened a fine dining restaurant called M, serving California cuisine, in Columbus. This strapped us even more for cash. I've always had a gift for turning two dollars into three by juggling funds, but the situation became extremely stressful. Most of our restaurants were profitable, but the relentless building of new locations was a cash-intensive undertaking. Sometimes, I had to close a loan to make payroll the next day.

9/11

I soon realized that I'd pushed people too far, not only physically, but also mentally. By doing too much, too fast, we'd compromised the soul of our company. Then came a catastrophe, and we had no financial cushion to soften the blow.

When I grasped the implications of the aircraft attacks on the United States on September 11th, I closed the company at 11:00 a.m., telling everyone to go home and be with their families and friends. I remember standing outside with my two children, wife, and neighbors gathered on the street, hugging and crying. We looked at the crystal blue skies and saw Air Force One fly over, the only plane allowed in the sky, escorted by two fighter jets. It brought a tear to my eye.

But we're Americans, and we weren't going to wallow. Even as we grieved for the massive loss of life, we had to go back to work the next day. I wanted to be open for our guests. Frankly, we needed to be open. I was worried about keeping the company afloat, preserving the jobs of all our associates, and facing the dire business reality that set in on September 12th. The government shut down the airlines; then a wave of anthrax powder attacks created more fear. Americans were transfixed by the crisis and not ready to resume their routines. As I feared, during the next two weeks, we saw the number of people visiting our restaurants plummeting. I knew business would take time to recover. The problem was that we didn't have much time, because we'd been spread so thin.

I was frightened, no doubt, but I believed failure was not an option for me. I faced the reality that we had to open four new restaurants within sixty days. The timing couldn't have been worse. However, construction was nearly complete, associates had been hired, and training was under way. There was no way to back out, and we had no choice except to forge ahead. Opening day was coming, whether we wanted it to or not.

David and Wayne went to Newport, Kentucky—a small upscale suburb just across the river from Cincinnati—to open a Mitchell's Fish Market. We ordinarily opened a restaurant with managers who knew our company and our culture inside and out. Our aggressive expansion schedule left us without enough experienced staff to send to the Newport location. We had to hire all the managers in that area, from outside our company. This meant that managers for the new location had to learn how to follow our culture as well as how to do their jobs. We sent the team to Columbus for eight weeks of training in our hometown restaurants, hoping we could instill the culture in that time, but we were sadly mistaken. It was impossible.

The Newport restaurant was soon in trouble, and not only because of the economy. A few months after we opened, we administered our associate opinion survey (AOS), and it became clear that we had failed to convey our principles and values to our staff. We failed to create raving fans of our associates and guests. Our new management team didn't comprehend what it meant to be great people delivering genuine hospitality, or *Yes is the answer. What is the question?*

The Louisville openings came next, and they weren't any easier. We opened two restaurants—a Mitchell's Fish Market and a Martini Italian Bistro—on the same day, October 26, 2001. For these openings, David and Wayne were out working their duffs off without much support. They got called for every problem. Anything and everything could happen, like the night David got a call from the manager of the hotel that was housing our training team: "We've just evicted your trainers. They were being too loud and rowdy." David had to get out of bed and find them another hotel in the middle of the night. This was just one of many endless difficulties he endured.

Meanwhile, back in Columbus, we went ahead with our long-planned Asian-themed restaurant, which we had designed as a competitor to P.F. Chang's. I named it Molly Woo's—after my wife, Molly, who had wooed me. (It was a cute play on words.) Though this restaurant is still open, successful, and profitable today, it became immediately clear that we knew little about Asian-themed restaurants, and we were not going to build a brand to compete with P.F. Chang's.

By the end of 2001, the shock of 9/11 began to ease, and our country started to resume normal business. I had learned a valuable lesson: mental and physical capital are as valuable as financial capital, and you can exhaust them at your peril. Our people were wiped out, and our finances were in turmoil. Our vendor payments were 120 days or more behind. We had a lot of work ahead to turn our company around and get healthy again.

When 2002 arrived, I had to introduce myself to the mirror and ask what I'd done—and what I needed to do to make it right. Leaders lead, I told myself, and I'd led us into this mess. Now I had to lead us out.

I visited all our purveyors for a personal talk, and told them the truth: it would take us a year to recover and make payments current again. I asked for their patience. It was a hat-in-hand moment. They were still struggling from 9/11, but everyone agreed and told me they'd be happy to help. I like to think that our long, positive relationships and our history of making raving fans of everyone we do business with strengthened their confidence in us.

FINDING FOCUS

Luckily, I had the benefit of some great advice.

I was in Las Vegas for a retreat with my forum of the Young Presidents' Organization. The YPO is organized in small groups called forums. Each forum comprises ten members, and these people become very close. One of my forum members, Larry Abbott, ran a big food distribution business, and was a key vendor for us. He pulled me aside one afternoon.

"Cameron, you seem like you're all over the board. Maybe you should just slow down a little bit and narrow your focus."

Around that time, a friend recommended I read *Good to Great,* a classic business book by Jim Collins. It was a transformative experience, and I gave copies to everyone on our executive leadership team.

Collins says the way to turn an enterprise from good to great is often not by doing many things well, but instead by doing one thing better than anyone else in the world. I often fall behind on my reading, but I gulped down *Good to Great* like a man who had run out of water in the desert. Our executive team and I had a vigorous discussion about the book, and carried out the exercises. It was at the convergence of these three questions that we would find our *Good to Great* strategy.

Where can you be number one or two in the marketplace?

What are you passionate about?

What can drive your economic engine?

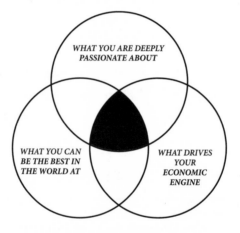

Our leadership team read Jim Collins's *Good to Great* on a tip from a mentor, and Collins's Hedgehog concept inspired us to refocus our strategy in the midst of the economic crisis after 9/11. Copyright© 2002.

Suddenly, the answer became clear to all of us. There was not another great seafood brand in the Midwest. No one had restaurants like Mitchell's Fish Market, which was popular and profitable. Plus, we were passionate about the brand, as we'd been among the first to bring fresh seafood dining to the Columbus area and other Midwest sites. We made our decision: We would build our expansion on the Fish Market brand. We now had a clear focus.

During this period of evolution, we also started to form discrete teams with defined responsibilities instead of everyone having their hands in everything.

A developer friend of mine was desperate for us to lease a site for a Mitchell's Fish Market in a new shopping center in Lansing, Michigan. He made us a deal we couldn't refuse, so in early 2002, we committed to opening a Fish Market there. Luckily, this store turned out to be a powerhouse. We also closed the Cap City Diner in Pittsburgh, two years after it opened, which was difficult but necessary. Sales had remained lackluster, and there was no parking. The result was zero net growth in the number of restaurants in 2002. We'd traded in a money loser in Pittsburgh for a highly profitable one in Lansing, and our cash flow perked up.

Yes, we'd crashed and fallen down the ski slope, and we had the feeling of lying in the snow with our goggles askew, hat lost, and ski poles twenty feet up the slope. We said we put associates first, but I'd worked our team too hard. Incidents such as the trainers partying all night in Louisville made it clear that our message wasn't reaching the entire staff. We'd expanded too fast to staff our new restaurants with managers instilled with our culture. We weren't yet living and breathing *Yes is the answer. What is the question?* in every nook and cranny of our company. Now, we knew what we needed to do.

And don't forget, 2002 was the year of the chocolate milkshake revelation described in the prologue—when we realized that our culture and core values weren't as ingrained and well-taught as they needed to be. Combined with our embrace of Jim Collins's *Good to Great* vision, this period became a real turning point in our company.

I looked for a way to say yes in 2002 to two more opportunities on our doorstep, which for many executives would have been easy *no's*. Catering was taking up a lot of our time, but generating only about 2 percent of CMR's revenue. We had to say yes to the charities, schools, and guests who wanted us to cater their special events. The requests kept coming and coming. I reached out to Melissa Johnson, who was general manager of our downtown Martini Restaurant at the time. I saw her as a go-getter with the entrepreneurial drive to grow the catering business.

I told Melissa, "I want to start this catering biz. I don't like to cater, but we need to do this. It needs to become an arm of our company so we can honor all the requests we're getting. Would you be interested in spearheading it?" She agreed, and launched the catering business under our flag. Cameron Mitchell Premier Events, as it is called today, now has as much annual revenue as our top restaurants.

The other opportunity involved one of my original investors, a friend of mine, Joe Miragliotta. We'd worked together as young bucks at the Cork & Cleaver. Joe came to see me at the end of 2001. He'd been laid off from his traveling telecom sales position, and he had a daughter with special needs who was getting older. Joe needed to work closer to home to support his daughter, and had the idea of opening a sports bar. I wasn't sure he had the personality and experience for it, but I said, "Joe, absolutely. I'll help you out."

I couldn't let Joe down. *No* was not the answer. I had to find a way to say *yes*. Then it hit me. I had another general manager, Gary Callicoat, who was also a friend, since I'd dated his sister for six years. Gary is like a brother to me. I often say that Gary's sister and I didn't work out—but Gary and I did. He and I were close enough that I wanted to get him out of the restaurants so we could partner on fun projects without opening myself to questions of favoritism.

I called them to a meeting and made introductions. "Listen, guys," I said. "I'd like to help you, but I can't open another restaurant right now. That will take my mental capital away from my partners, who have invested in us at a hard time and need my full attention. Joe, you need someone with experience. Gary, you need to run a place of your own outside of CMR. I think we can create a separate company under the guidance of CMR. Our CMR team will do your accounting, site selection, purchasing, marketing, and so forth. You guys can run the day-to-day operations. CMR will charge the new company a small percentage of sales as a management fee, and a take a piece of the sale price if the brand ever sells."

We all agreed, and built the first Rusty Bucket in Dublin, Ohio, as a neighborhood corner tavern with made-from-scratch food, a family-friendly atmosphere, and multiple televisions for watching sports—with the sound off, mind you.

By this point, later in 2002, I saw a breakthrough coming, and felt more optimistic. We'd reorganized and launched new ventures. I knew the value of our people and our culture, and I had learned some critical lessons. Also, I had turned forty, and Molly and I had moved into our new house in the Upper Arlington neighborhood in Columbus. I was humbled and overjoyed when Molly gave birth to our daughter and third child, Bonnie Louise. Our family was complete, and the future was bright.

OPERATION *GOOD TO GREAT*

–

2003-2008

We began 2003 armed with our new focus and our *Good to Great* strategy. We had learned from our mistakes, and we had returned to what mattered and what was non-negotiable—our culture and values. The whole management team was on board to build our Mitchell's Fish Market brand for the next however-many years to come. Our daily mantra—push the flywheel—kept us moving forward. Every push made things happen, as Jim Collins described so well:

> *You keep pushing, and the flywheel begins to move a bit faster, and with continued great effort, you move it around a second rotation. You keep pushing in a consistent direction. Three turns... four... five... six... The flywheel builds up speed... seven... eight... You keep pushing... nine... ten... It builds momentum... eleven... twelve... moving faster with each turn... twenty... thirty... fifty... a hundred.*

*Then, at some point—breakthrough! The mo-
mentum of the thing kicks in your favor, hurling
the flywheel forward, turn after turn... whoosh!...
its own heavy weight working for you. You're pushing no harder than during the first rotation, but the
flywheel goes faster and faster. Each turn of the flywheel builds upon work done earlier, compounding
your investment of effort. A thousand times faster,
then ten thousand, then a hundred thousand. The
huge, heavy disk flies forward, with almost unstop-
pable momentum.*

— Jim Collins, *Good to Great*

Early in this new phase, I had a major revelation about the Mitchell's Fish Market brand. I was in Kentucky, visiting one of the original
six restaurants. It was a slow night, but when I stepped outside and
looked across the street at a Brio Tuscan Grille, I couldn't help but
notice that they were a whole lot busier than we were. Their crowd
was younger, and their design was modern and warm. I looked at our
restaurant with new eyes. It had been designed with an East Coast
blue and nautical theme; the intention was to give the feeling of Cape
Cod or Maine. As I looked at the stone tile floors and cobalt color, I
suddenly saw that the decor was staid and cold, and it had to change.
The look and feel of the brand needed a redesign.

After a nationwide search, I interviewed some great restaurant de-
signers, including Mark Knauer, based in Chicago. Mark delivered a
presentation that was so good, I went on my gut and told him on the
spot that he was hired.

"What do you mean, I'm hired?"

"I like you. I think you'll do a great job for us."

"Don't you want to see a proposal?" He looked at me in shock.

I told him that I didn't need a bid. "I trust your pencil is going to be sharp, because you want to design more restaurants with us in the future. I'm sure your price will be good." We sealed the deal, and Mark has designed nearly all our restaurants ever since.

BUILDING THE FISH MARKET BRAND
AND PUSHING THE FLYWHEEL

We signed leases to open five new Fish Markets in 2003 and 2004. The first would be in Birmingham, Michigan, an affluent Detroit suburb. I chose Detroit because I'd heard great things about the market, including comments from one of my best buddies who lived up there. We selected a site on a ring road that looped around the back of the main boulevard. Several people advised us that this location was better than the main drag because everyone used the ring road to go places. At first, I was skeptical. It seemed counterintuitive, but I went out and studied it. Yes, it was true—all traffic went around that ring road, so I decided to give it a shot.

In May 2003, we opened our doors in Birmingham and launched our new, warmer design. The new colors were burgundy, cream, and brass. As with the prior design, you knew you were in a seafood restaurant, but now you were more likely to think of the Gulf Coast, the Carolinas, or perhaps California. The feeling was modern and plush, but comfortable.

Unfortunately, the first week was slower than molasses, and I beat myself up thinking we'd made a terrible mistake. However, the following week picked up, and the week after that, we were even busier. Restaurants can be that way. Some open immediately hot, while others open slowly and build momentum—which is exactly what happened. By December, the new restaurant became our number-one Fish Market, bringing in record sales of more than $100,000 a week.

Birmingham was a great start, and we kept pushing that flywheel. Four months later, we opened a Mitchell's Fish Market in Woodmere, Ohio—a Cleveland suburb with a strong reputation as the area's upscale shopping and dining mecca. In 2004, we opened three more Mitchell's Fish Markets, all similarly placed in shopping centers of well-to-do suburbs. One of these was in West Chester, Ohio, on the major route between Cincinnati and Dayton; the next in Glenview, a booming town just north of Chicago. After that came Carmel, just outside Indianapolis. All of them did well, and we knew we were onto something.

Why did we succeed? It wasn't just one thing; it was many. Our food was excellent, as always. The location was right: a dense, wealthy suburb full of people who appreciated fine food. And our new design was great. Most importantly, we recommitted to our culture and values. I can't emphasize that enough. Staying true to our culture was and still is the key to our success. This time, we opened all of our new restaurants with experienced, homegrown people in senior management positions, and we strengthened our cadre of Columbus-based trainers, who went on the road to shape the local staff. This was critical. Our trainers are the true ambassadors who pass on our culture and values to new associates.

The reviewers became raving fans, too. An *Indianapolis Monthly* critic swooned over our Lobster Bisque, our Chilean Sea Bass, and our Shanghai Salmon steamed with ginger and scallions. Our Shark Fin Pie was a huge hit: a big triangular dessert wedge made with peanut butter, chocolate, ice cream, and an Oreo® cookie crust. It looked like a shark's fin as it sailed through the dining room on a tray carried by our associates, turning heads as it went.

All five of the new Fish Markets were thriving, so we decided to remodel our six original restaurants, which were still decorated in the old nautical blue scheme. Sales increased.

Even at this time, as we pushed the flywheel and focused, we made two departures from our *Good to Great* plan. The first was initiated by our landlord in Birmingham, Michigan. The Fish Market there stood at the base of a condo tower, and right next to it was a 6,500-square-foot empty space. The landlord invited us to build a steakhouse there—he knew we had a successful steakhouse in Columbus. He offered the same lease deal that we had next door.

I thought about it, and was intrigued. Our Fish Market was doing great there, and I looked around and did not see any other steakhouses in town. When I learned we wouldn't need a second $750,000 liquor license, I was even more interested. According to the state liquor authority, as long as our two restaurants were physically connected, they would be considered one contiguous space and could share the original liquor license. All I had to do was cut a door between the two restaurants.

Since the landlord had provided the liquor license as part of our first lease, I held him to his promise to give us the same deal on the second, and asked him to credit $750,000 toward our build-out. He agreed, and as a result, we were able to open that restaurant at relatively little cost. We called it Cameron's Steakhouse. The design was sleek and beautiful, and it exuded welcoming warmth. The steakhouse opened like a house on fire. Before long, it was one of the busiest places in downtown Birmingham, bringing in more than $100,000 a week, just like its sister restaurant next door.

The steakhouse detour didn't slow down our overall plan. We were still in *Good to Great* mode. By 2005, we had opened another Mitchell's Fish Market in Pittsburgh, followed in 2006 by Fish Markets in Tampa, Florida and Rochester Hills, Michigan, another Detroit-area location.

A COOK NAMED MARCELLA

Then came the second detour. David Miller, our president and chief operating officer, had Italian food on his mind after he visited a wonderful Italian restaurant in Chicago that was packed to the rafters. He came back saying, "Man, we've got to open up something like this in Columbus." Not long after, he told me about a location: a cool storefront restaurant site had become available in the Short North District, an up-and-coming arts neighborhood in Columbus.

I liked the idea. It so happened that my family had been going to Italy for years. We'd rented the same villa in Tuscany many times, and I'd fallen in love with authentic Italian cooking, the region's beauty, and the way of life.

We questioned whether we should deviate once again from Operation *Good to Great* and open an Italian restaurant, but we concluded that our difficulties were, by then, five years in the rearview mirror, and we'd righted the ship. Anyway, this was just a slight departure from our strategy, we reasoned. After all, we were a multi-concept restaurant company, right? Plus, we thought it would be fun.

So we developed a new concept—a rustic Italian trattoria with a beautiful wooden bar, hanging globe lights, and a casual feeling. The menu focused on uncomplicated food—pizza, pasta dishes, antipasti, cured meats, soups, and salads—done well in the simple Italian tradition.

Sometimes, naming restaurants can be very difficult; at other times it's easy. In this case, it was a breeze. I wanted a name that would pay homage to the pure flavors of Italy. Immediately, I thought of Marcella Libertini, my favorite Italian cook. Marcella was the chef and house manager at the villa where my family and I had stayed a number of times in the Val d'Orcia region of Tuscany, and we'd built a very nice rapport with her over the years. She'd baked cookies with our kids and taught my wife and her friends how to roll pasta. She had always gone the extra mile and demonstrated extraordinary hospitality. Even though my wife and I didn't speak Italian and Marcella didn't speak English, we talked in the kitchen at the villa each day, using sign language and pointing to words in the Italian-English dictionary. I thought it would be perfect to name the restaurant after her. Our executive team loved the idea. A few years earlier, I'd brought them to Tuscany to celebrate our company's tenth anniversary, so they'd met Marcella and experienced her cooking and hospitality firsthand.

Once we agreed to name the restaurant Marcella's, I wanted to bring the real Marcella to the opening. The logistics were complicated for a woman who did not speak English, and, to my knowledge, might never have ventured as far as Rome. I contacted John Bird, who provided concierge services for guests at the villa and spoke fluent Italian in addition to English. We'd gotten to know and trust him over the years, so I asked if he would be willing to escort Marcella to the States, and he agreed. When he asked Marcella if she would like to be our guest, she started to cry. "Oh, my God. I would love to go to the United States. I have never been."

John said, "I'm going to take you. Mr. Mitchell is opening another restaurant, and he is going to name it after you."

When word spread that Marcella was having a restaurant in the United States named after her and the owner was flying her in for the opening, she became a bit of a celebrity in her village. I don't know what I was thinking when I arranged for her and John to spend their first few nights in the U.S. at the Marriott Times Square in Manhattan. Needless to say, the culture shock made her head spin, and she was overwhelmed at first. She quickly acclimated though, going on shopping expeditions and returning to the hotel weighed down by bags of purchases. John remembered this in vivid detail, because he was the one carrying all the bags. Marcella and John then traveled up to the Culinary Institute of America, where I had arranged a grand tour and gave her the opportunity to do a cooking demo for the students. She loved it.

When Marcella finally reached Columbus, I wasted no time before taking her to the restaurant. No translations were needed to understand how she felt when she saw her name over the door. Her beaming face and tears made it obvious she was ecstatic. We took many pictures together that day, then brought her behind the line and put an apron on her. She gave a cooking class for the staff, making eggplant *caponata* and half-moon-shaped ravioli, both of which we put on the restaurant menu. The chefs and kitchen staff stood in a circle around her, watching in awe.

Marcella loved the restaurant, the people, and the United States. "I always had a dream to come to America," she said on opening night. She loved our hometown, too. "Columbus is so much nicer a place than New York," she told a reporter for *The Columbus Dispatch*.

Marcella Libertini, the Italian chef and restaurant namesake, cooked with the chefs at Marcella's in the Short North neighborhood of Columbus, 2007.

To cap off the trip, I wanted to extend to Marcella the same sort of hospitality she'd shown my family. One summer, when we were at the villa on the Fourth of July, she had arranged for fireworks and made apple pie with vanilla gelato. I've never forgotten that special holiday touch, which was so near and dear to my heart. On her last night, my wife Molly and I had Marcella over to our house along with several close friends and family. She had created so many wonderful Italian meals for us, and I wanted to return the favor and show American favorites to her. Our catering team prepared a feast of every American classic you could imagine: barbecued ribs, baked beans, fried chicken, burgers, corn on the cob, sheet cake, strawberry shortcake, and more. She was elated, and we were thrilled to do it.

Of course, the trip was expensive—but whatever money we spent paled in comparison with the goodwill we received for our company. It was another example that when you do the right thing, good comes back to you. Our Marcella's staff gained a deeper understanding of what we were trying to do with the restaurant, and the media coverage we received was priceless publicity because of Marcella's warm, wonderful presence. But I didn't do it to receive goodwill or great PR. I did it for Marcella, who had been so good to our family— and that was reason enough.

RUTH'S CHRIS AND THE SALE OF A LIFETIME

By the middle of 2006, we had been working on our *Good to Great* plan for several years. All the Mitchell's Fish Markets were remodeled in the new design, and sales were great. The steakhouse in Birmingham was killing it for us. Marcella's was killing it for us. We also remodeled our Mitchell's Ocean Club in Columbus, and doing so boosted sales to $6.5 million just serving dinner, versus $4.4 million before the renovation for lunch *and* dinner.

Yes, things were going great. The problem was that the company was still carrying $20 million in debt, and I was personally guaranteed on all of it. I didn't want this stress anymore. When I learned that my friends Rick and Chris Doody—whom I'd known since middle school—had sold just their Bravo Brio Restaurant Group for $170 million, I went up to see Chris at his lake house in Michigan in the fall of 2006. That day we spoke about his experience selling his company. I asked how he felt about it and picked his brain. Naturally, he was flush with cash and felt great.

As I described to him our plans for opening more restaurants and considered my debt, it suddenly became clear that what Chris and his brother had done would be the perfect scenario for us. It hit me like a ton of bricks. We should sell the Mitchell's Fish Market brand to a major company with the capacity to grow the brand faster than we could.

This way, our Fish Market associates would have better opportunities to rise and succeed, and we would have the capital to pay off debt, reward our investors, and build more restaurants, like Ocean Prime and Marcella's. Our whole company could grow more quickly.

In December 2006, we quietly hired the investment banking and asset-management firm of Piper Jaffray, recommended by Chris, to manage the sale. On a freezing cold, snowy day, David Miller, Diane Smullen, Stacey Connaughton, and I flew up to Detroit to meet with them at our Birmingham Fish Market. We had a great discussion that day, and left with a realistic understanding of what the sale would take. There would be thousands of hours preparing for meetings with bankers and buyers, but I thought it was doable. The first and most important step was to create a confidential information memorandum, which was an enormous document that would tell our story, describe each restaurant location, and provide financials, photos, and a boatload of other metrics. By the end of the first quarter of 2007, we had this eighty-page beast done. Technically, we were ready to go to market, but after doing some homework, we decided to wait.

The reason was that when I looked back at the previous year, I saw we'd had a not-so-good second quarter in 2006, and this reduced our EBITDA (earnings before interest, taxes, depreciation, and amortization), which is essentially net profit for the prior twelve months. This is one of the most important metrics in determining the value of a company. Usually, the total acquisition price of a restaurant company is about nine times the EBITDA. I wanted to wait ninety days before going to market, so the second quarter of 2006 would drop out of the picture and the most recent quarter would be included, instead. Also, we were scheduled to open four new Fish Markets in 2007, and I expected these new revenue streams to boost our numbers.

Another huge push of the flywheel. That spring, we opened a Fish Market in Brookfield, Wisconsin, just outside Milwaukee, and another in Sandestin, Florida, on the Gulf Coast. The reviews were great.

"Price and quality intersect at a pleasant point at Mitchell's," wrote one Milwaukee-area writer who raved about the high-quality food, the bustling atmosphere, and the service, which was "as attentive as at any fine dining restaurant in Milwaukee."

Sales were great, too. We booked a fantastic second quarter in 2007 and increased our EBITDA from $7.9 million to $8.9 million—a $1 million increase from ninety days earlier.

Now we were ready.

In July 2007, Piper Jaffray took us to market. Ruth's Hospitality Group quickly came to the table. Between their franchise and corporate restaurants, they were a $600 million company with aspirations of reaching $1 billion in annual sales. With the acquisition of our Fish Market brand, Ruth's goal was to add another growth vehicle for themselves and their franchisees.

Naturally, there were months of push and pull. Ruth's Hospitality Group, which owns the steakhouse chain Ruth's Chris, was concerned that with the cash from the sale in our pockets, we might start building steakhouses and create competition for them. When they asked us to agree to a lengthy non-compete period, I suggested they buy our three existing steakhouses as part of the deal. After many negotiations, we agreed to the price of $94 million for all nineteen Fish Markets and our three steakhouses. This represented 10.3 times our EBITDA, which was a strong offer. In November 2007, we signed the purchase agreement and planned to close in early 2008.

In retrospect, I can see the perfect timing of the deal. If we'd gone to market ninety days earlier, we would have gotten about $10 million less in sale price. If we had waited one more quarter to go to market, I doubt the sale would have happened at all. No one foresaw (or wanted to see) the extraordinary economic crash that was coming. By late 2007, the economy was showing cracks. We were scheduled to close on the deal in February 2008. By then, Ruth's Chris stock was starting to drop, and days before the close, they tried to back out of the deal. For us, this was impossible. We had spent more than a million dollars to get ready for the sale.

"If you break this contract, I am going to start a new company dedicated solely to suing you for damages and breach of contract," I told the chairman of Ruth's Chris. He got the message. Ultimately, we gave back $2 million and had a deal. The final document contained non-compete agreements. It also stipulated that our company would stay on as an advisor for the first year after the sale, so we could transfer our expertise and culture to Ruth's Chris.

On February 19, 2008, a text message vibrated on my phone amid a meeting of my Young Presidents' Organization forum group. It was from Diane, who wrote, "The money has been wired to our account. The deal is done."

To say that we were overjoyed would be a vast understatement. I was awash with emotions and revelations. I felt true jubilation. Still, it was bittersweet to say goodbye to our Fish Markets, which so many had given so much to build. I felt anxiety at all the public attention that was sure to come from news coverage of the sale. Life would never be the same.

In the coming weeks, there were many parties and celebrations, but the first was a complete surprise. On the night of the closing, I came home to find that Molly had gathered friends and neighbors to surprise me and celebrate the sale. It was a beautiful night, and I was overwhelmed by her gesture. She had always been there to support me, day in and day out, all those years. I never could have done it without her.

SHARING THE WEALTH

Our stellar growth from 2003 through 2007 had been a wall-to-wall winning streak—a phenomenal, heart-pounding success made possible by the dedication, hard work, and sacrifices our team had made every working hour of every day. There had been eighty-hour workweeks, late-night, long-distance drives home from new locations, moments of doubt, and an extraordinary amount of administrative work and midnight oil burned during the three months preceding the sale.

It was extremely important to me to share our windfall with the managers who had given so much. I distributed 5 percent of the sale price—$4.6 million—in bonuses to the company leadership, including restaurant managers, executive chefs, and our home office team. In addition, several people owned stock they'd earned through sweat equity. These operating partners, as we called them, owned 5 percent of the company stock, and they collectively earned several million dollars more. It was a good day for everyone.

As for me, I paid off all my personal debt and our company debt. I also bought out some partners. We now had $3 million in cash and an untouched, $6-million line of credit. For the company, it was a clean slate. As for me personally, I had about $10 million cash in the bank.

One night, when the sale was nearing, I woke up thinking about our executive team: the eight people who had worked so hard for so long. They and their families had made many sacrifices over the years. Several had been with me for more than a decade. I wanted to say thank you to each of them in a more personal way—something from me, not the company.

I got out of bed, went to my desk, and began writing cards to the eight executives, describing my gift to each. I tried to choose things and experiences that would be perfect not only for each team member, but also for his or her family. Diane, our CFO, had spent countless late nights at the office not seeing her husband while we worked on the deal. She had talked about wanting to take her husband to Tennessee's Blackberry Farm someday. On her card, I wrote that I would fly the couple on a private jet for a three-day, all-expenses-paid trip to Blackberry Farm so they could reconnect. For the year or two prior, David, our president and COO, had told me on numerous occasions that his wife wanted a brand-new Mini Cooper. On his card, I wrote: *This gift isn't really for you (though it is). Have your wife go and pick out a brand-new Mini Cooper from you, on me.* For Jim Torski, our VP of operations who worried about getting three kids through college, I promised the first year's tuition for each at Ohio State University or the equivalent. To Stacey, my longstanding assistant, I gave $25,000 in company stock, because I wanted her to own more of the company that she had helped me build from day one.

For their celebration, the executive team didn't want to do anything audacious or grandiose—no thousand-dollar bottles of champagne. They wanted to have fun. While we trudged through the months, preparing for the sale, they decided that if this deal went through, we'd all celebrate by going out for burgers and beers followed by bowling. It was the exact opposite of what people would have expected, and I thought it was a great idea.

We went out to the Press Grill, all of us wearing bowling shirts that Jim had custom-made with fun nicknames sewn on each person's pocket. When the burgers were finished and we were having another beer, I said, "There's one more thing."

That was when I handed the envelopes to each team member. I asked them to read their cards aloud, one at a time. It might have seemed like a strange thing to do, but each gift was so different and meaningful that I wanted them to share the experience with one another. Of course, there was shock, awe, a few tears, and a lot of hugs. It was one of the proudest moments of my career.

An unforgettable day. The executive team celebrated with burgers, beer, and bowling upon the sale of the Mitchell's Fish Market and Steakhouse restaurants to Ruth's Chris which was consummated February 2008.

The team later reciprocated, creating a beautiful photo book for me filled with images of themselves and their families enjoying the gifts along with heartfelt notes of thanks that I will always cherish. "It was unexpected and truly touching for you to show how much you care for us," said one. "In the same way that I feel you would do anything for us, I want you to know my loyalty to you shows no bounds.

If there is anything you ever need, I would always be there to help."
They also gave me a second gift—a plaque. This plaque depicted a
donation of $5,000 a year to the Ohio State University Hospitality
Management School for five years, for scholarships in my name paid
for by our executive team. It was a very touching moment for me,
and totally unexpected. It brought me to tears.

There were many team celebrations and parties. A group of us
took the leadership team of the Fish Markets for a celebration at the
MGM Grand Hotel in Detroit. We had a blast, though it was a bittersweet farewell for those who would be leaving to work for Ruth's
Chris. We felt confident that they would be going to a good place,
because Ruth's Chris had so many more resources than we did to
grow the brand.

It was the spring of 2008. I was forty-five years old—still in my
prime, fired up, and ready to launch again. We had built forty-plus
restaurants, and had just sold twenty-two of them for $92 million.
Despite having sold two-thirds of our business, we did not lay anyone off at the home office. Without flinching, I immediately wanted
to rebuild. I had forgotten how tough those ten years had been. I'd
forgotten it immediately and completely.

Our deal made national headlines in the restaurant industry. It
closed right as the economic boom of the early 2000s faltered, and
the first whispers of 2008's financial collapse sounded in the distance.

7

THE BIG FALL

–

2008-2012

All through the spring of 2008, I was on cloud nine. I had a satchel of money in the bank, and I was flying around on private planes. Our restaurants were doing great. Our people were doing great. Everything was great. With all this greatness, I was certain we could rebuild within two to three years what originally had taken us ten to create. From the moment we signed the agreement with Ruth's Chris until several months after we closed the deal, I went on a tear, signing leases for seven new restaurants to be built within eighteen months. The expected cost: $22 million.

Let me repeat that: seven restaurants in eighteen months. $22 million.

I don't know how to explain my stupidity and arrogance, other than to say I allowed the euphoria of our success to delude me. "We'll be even bigger next time," I said to the executive team. I poured it on, pulled them in with me, and got everyone in the mood. Even the naysayers didn't have a chance. Then I circulated a piece of paper and asked everyone for their sales projections on the seven new restaurants. We tallied the votes. All of our estimates were fairly close to one another, averaging an anticipated $45 million.

We planned to do a *Good to Great* campaign all over again—except this time, we would focus on a new brand, Ocean Prime, inspired by our Ocean Club restaurant in Columbus. It was a glamorous white-tablecloth concept with superb seafood and prime-cut steaks. The atmosphere was beautiful and dramatic—a supper club with a piano bar and servers wearing white jackets. Just as we'd done with Mitchell's Fish Markets, we would build a bunch of them, and who knew, maybe we'd make a big sale once again.

We chose Troy, Michigan, a suburb of Detroit, for our first location and called upon our architect, Mark Knauer, who delivered a stunning design that we built from the ground up. The building had a semicircular façade wrapped in a white band, with *Ocean Prime* emblazoned over the doors. You couldn't help but turn your head when you drove past it. The interior had floor-to-ceiling windows, dramatic chandeliers, and warm wood tones. There was a hint of art deco.

From the moment it opened, the place was on fire. We got great reviews, and started taking in about $200,000 a week. I was fired up because we were killing it. We had six more restaurants to go. It was June 2008, and we charged ahead and began construction on three more Ocean Primes, all to open during the fourth quarter of 2008 in Miami, Florida; Phoenix, Arizona; and Orlando, Florida, respectively.

In August, these three projects were well under way when my CFO, Diane Smullen, came into my office and shut the door behind her. It was time for a check-in.

"How are we doing in cash?" I asked, as I always do.

Her face looked serious.

"It's getting tight," she said, with more than a little gravity in her voice.

"What do you mean, it's getting tight?"

"We've burned through our $3 million in cash, and we've used most of our $6 million line of credit."

"How can that be?"

"We had a ton of payables left over from the sale, we just built Ocean Prime Troy, and we've got three restaurants under construction."

"Listen. It'll be okay," I reassured her. "We're going to earn more money. We're going to be fine."

"Well, it's tight," she repeated.

"Sure," I said.

And that was that.

Diane is an incredible chief financial officer and a person of extreme integrity. But I knew it was her job to be conservative, and at that moment, I did not want her caution to interfere with my optimism. So I pushed away any worry, telling myself I had a lot of money in the bank.

Gift-certificate season would soon be there to refill our coffers.

The three new restaurants would soon be doing very well, I was sure of it.

I'd do whatever I had to do.

One month later, the global financial crisis hit. Suddenly, everything looked quite a bit different. During that September of economic shock, I found myself glued to CNBC, watching the events unfold. The housing bubble had burst, Lehman Brothers had collapsed, and Congress was debating a $700-billion bank bailout. At the end of the month, the stock market sank nearly eight hundred points in a single day. Then came the massive layoffs. The Great Recession had arrived, and it felt as if the sky had fallen.

Almost overnight, our superstar Ocean Prime in Troy, Michigan, dropped 25 percent in sales. Meanwhile, I was completely leveraged with three expensive restaurants scheduled to open within a couple months. Americans were losing their jobs and their homes, and they were not going out to eat.

Somehow, we got those three restaurants open. Our original projections called for them to do about $22 million a year. They did about half of that. We started losing money immediately. By the end of 2008, we'd fallen behind with our vendors—over 90 days past due.

Thanks to the decline of the stock market, the $10 million I'd personally received from the sale was now worth between $6 million and $7 million. I had no choice but to draw upon it, bit by bit in the coming months, and put much of it back into the company to stabilize the business. I turned to friends who agreed to lend me $3 million, and together we made a $7 million mezzanine loan to the business that would stabilize the company while we finished opening these restaurants and waited for the recession to end.

Unfathomably, we were committed to opening Ocean Prime number five in Tampa, Florida right before Super Bowl weekend of 2009. Defying the trend, this new location turned out to be an absolute home run. Even with the recession, it came out of the starting gates super-strong, with a mid-sized city rent but a big-city volume of guests. Sales were gunning at a rate of $10 million a year, and it was a godsend. Tampa was the buoy that kept us afloat. It infused cash into the company with a $2 million-a-year profit.

In April, we usually give our associates pay raises—typically 5 percent,—but in 2009, we had to tell everyone there would be no raises that year. Considering the state of the economy—everyone knew someone who'd lost a job or taken a pay cut—our people were understanding. Nevertheless, the announcement sowed the seeds of worry. I'll never forget the moment when Stacey Connaughton came into my office a few months later and told me there was scuttlebutt around our central office that layoffs probably would follow. As soon as I got wind of this, I asked for an all-staff meeting to be held in five minutes. Open, honest communication is one of our core values. This was a moment when people really needed to know what was going on and to hear from me personally.

EMBRACING OUR CULTURE AND
VALUES MORE DEEPLY IN CRISIS

When everyone had gathered in the conference room, I looked out at their faces and could see the worry.

"I understand that there are some rumors that people are going to be laid off," I began. "Well, I'm not going to make any bones about it; we're having a tough time. We are down to about $1.5 million in profit, and we have a $10 million loan. In the banking world, that's a troubled loan. But when times are tough, you don't throw the culture out the window—that's when you embrace it even more deeply. You know the part of the culture that says the associates come first? That's still alive and well."

"Right now, we are spending $700,000 annually on advertising and marketing. I assure you all that I will cut the advertising budget before I cut the people budget. So all you have to do is come to work and ask Carolyn Delp, our VP of marketing at the time, if we are still advertising. If we are, then you know there will be no layoffs."

"If I cut the advertising and we still need to cut something else after that, I will. But if, at some point, there is nothing else I can cut and we need to trim more, I'll give you all the choice. I'll call a meeting and say that we need to save, for example, another

$500,000 a year, and that's a 6 percent to 7 percent pay cut for everybody, or it means letting six people go. Then I'll leave the room and let you vote. And when I come back—if I'm a betting man, and I am—I'll bet that you all will vote to take a pay cut rather than to lay anyone off."

"After that's implemented, if it's *still* not enough, I will call another meeting, and I will tell you that we need to cut, say, eight people, and I'll let you know on Monday who it's going to be. When Monday comes, I'm going to walk into the office of each and every one of those eight people and talk to them personally. Then I'll give each a hug, hold the door open for them on the way out, and assure them I'm going to get them back as soon as I can."

"So until I have that meeting, no one is getting laid off. With that said, we need all hands on deck. We need you. And if you have an idea to save money—whether it's a dollar or a hundred thousand dollars—send it to me. I want to know about it. Now's the time we need to dig in and work hard, so let's get back to work and be awesome. We'll get through this all together."

After that conversation, our people went back to their desks, all fired up. They sent me dozens of ideas. They worked harder and smarter than ever, because they knew what was at stake. This was our culture and values in action.

Unfortunately, things were going to get worse before they got better.

A few months later, in August 2009, I had a "near-death experience" when I was out playing golf with a friend. We were at my private club, where cell phones were prohibited, and at the seventeenth hole, I looked up and saw a golf cart coming toward me. The manager was driving it, and he was holding a cell phone.

"It's Stacey. She says it's an emergency."

My stomach fell as I took the phone. Her voice was calm, but clearly upset.

"Cam, the bank has just called our credit," she said.

"I'll come to the office now." I left the golf course immediately.

In my car on the way over, I called Stacey back and had her read to me, word for word, the letter she'd just received from the bank. In the end it said that they were not asking us to pay back the entire $6 million line of credit and $4 million for equipment leases all at once, as I'd feared, but that they were freezing our credit. This was a very different thing—but not good at all. The bank had brought in a new chairman recently, and I had no relationship with him. I had one remaining influential friend there, so I called him up. He looked into our situation and discovered that some incorrect information had led to the freezing of our credit. Within an hour, it was fixed.

The experience scared the hell out of me. It was an era when banks were under enormous pressure from regulators to write off bad debt so they could clean up their balance sheets. We were at serious risk of having our line of credit shut down, because our debt-to-income ratio was not healthy at the time. If we hadn't had such a good reputation in the community, and if I hadn't had a friend high up in the bank, who knew what could have happened?

DARK TIMES

Two more restaurants to go: a Marcella's in Scottsdale, Arizona, and our sixth Ocean Prime in Dallas, Texas. These would cost $8 million. We were tight with cash and had no more room on our credit line. I had to face the prospect of going to our partners and investors to raise funds. This was an incredibly painful and humiliating experience. A year earlier, we had been celebrating our big sale to

Ruth's Chris. Plenty of people thought I'd kept the whole $92 million and was rolling in dough. No one understood why I would be back seeking new investment capital in the company. People were skeptical, and it did not go well. I tried to raise $14 million to build the restaurants and pay down our line, but could manage only about $9 million, including my own last $5 million. With Tampa doing so well and the new infusion of capital secured, we were able to survive.

During this troubling period, the hardest thing of all was looking in the mirror and facing my own hubris. I realized I'd made some of the same mistakes as in 2000 and 2001, when we'd expanded too rapidly and stretched ourselves too thin. I had accepted those mistakes as a learning experience. We'd recovered, and gone on to great success. Why hadn't I learned those lessons better? How could I have plummeted us into the same mess in such a short time, forcing me to take the money I'd made from the sale and plow it back into the company? I was personally broke. The only assets I had were tied up in the company.

Just as in our prior overexpansion, we were opening so many restaurants in such a short time that we didn't have enough home-grown staff to lead the new associates. We had to hire managers from outside the company. Just like the last time, the newcomers could not learn our culture in a few weeks of training. And just like the last time, restaurant performance suffered as a result.

"It took some shitty entrepreneuring to get us into this situation, and it's going to take some great entrepreneuring to get us out of it." This was what I told our executive team to lift them up, and I believed it, but I was living with fear and regret continually weighing on my gut.

I tried to shield my wife, Molly, from as much of it as I could. When I ran out of my own money, I took out a loan from a friend at

10 percent interest so I could maintain my family's lifestyle. I could not afford to take money out of the company to pay myself. I did not tell her directly how bad it was, but she felt me sleeping feverishly, and she saw me getting up in the middle of the night to scratch numbers on paper. Of course, she knew.

We had two restaurants to open during the fall of 2009, which would complete our seven-restaurant, eighteen-month expansion—for better or worse. Then we'd crawl to the holiday season, which always brought an infusion of cash with gift card sales and holiday diners. We just had to hold on. In 2010, we hoped, people would get back to work, and the economy would pick up.

That was the plan, but it didn't quite go that way. On that optimistic day in the conference room when we'd all scribbled our annual sales projections on a piece of paper, our average estimate had been $45 million for seven new restaurants. In reality, annualized sales at these restaurants were about $30 million.

Marcella's Scottsdale was a head-on disaster. I knew it the night I arrived for the orientation.

It is a tradition that I, personally, always lead orientations for our new restaurant openings and it is extremely important to me for so many reasons. I talk about our company culture and values, and I personally connect with our people. After the event, we take out the lead trainers and opening management team for dinner and drinks, and usually, the night is a great time. Having fun and bonding together is an important part of our DNA, so I want our associates to experience this right from the start.

But the orientation in Scottsdale was excruciating for me. As soon as I arrived, I could see that we'd made a grave mistake. The restaurant was located in a new shopping center, and it was dead. We took the staff out to the restaurant next door, and that was dead, too. The reality was sinking in that we'd opened a 10,000-square-foot pasta restaurant in the middle of a desert. It was clear that I had signed these deals with such hubris that I had not done my homework or carried out due diligence.

A couple of months later, in November 2009, Ocean Prime in Dallas opened extremely strong, and this helped us greatly, but Marcella's in Scottsdale kept dragging us down.

One thing was sure: we would open no new restaurants for at least a year, and we would take that time to retrench. We were all contemplating Jim Collins's *Good to Great* model, and we weren't going to give up on growth. We believed in the Ocean Prime brand. Tampa continued to be a superstar performer—today, it does $15 million a year—and our first Ocean Prime in Troy, Michigan had stabilized. Two of the other three locations—Phoenix and Miami—were not doing so well, but that was because of the poor locations, not a reflection of the brand.

I saw no way forward other than to continue building the brand.

That was why, when my real estate broker told me about a rare opportunity in downtown Denver, I listened. A very special space had become available at Fifteenth and Larimer, a prominent corner in Larimer Square, a vibrant historic district near all kinds of cultural landmarks. I loved it. It was the kind of lease you are ecstatic to sign. At the end of 2009, we accepted the agreement, and planned to open a year later. In fact, construction took a bit longer, so we opened in Denver in January 2011, making 2010 our first year in company history that we hadn't opened any new restaurants. It was a good thing to have this break.

As expected, Denver opened incredibly strong.

The big problem was still Marcella's in Scottsdale. This restaurant lost $100,000 the first month after it opened, and $100,000 every month after that. We'd spent more than $3 million to build it, and once a year had passed, it clearly wasn't going to perform any better. We were paying $600,000 a year in rent, plus operating expenses. We had to cut our losses and move on.

I went to the landlord and asked to get out of the lease, but that went nowhere fast. He wanted millions to let us go. I consulted with my attorneys—read: paid them $50,000—and asked them to "find a crease in the lease" so I could get out. They reviewed the document, but could find no potential exits. They offered to look deeper into the negotiations in their entirety to see what, if anything, they might find. Considering the fact that I was facing millions in losses, what was an extra $25,000? I said yes.

After an archeological dig into our correspondence for this deal— thanks to Keith Rogers, our real estate broker, who keeps each and every email for every deal he does—the lawyers found something remarkable: an email I had long forgotten. It turned out that back in the first week of September 2008, I'd emailed the leasing agent, saying that I wasn't sure I wanted to go forward, given the shaky economy. He had replied that Scottsdale was "recession-proof," and this location was a slam-dunk. I said we needed better assurances than that, and we would sign the deal only if they could share with me the current sales volume for each of the restaurants in the center. Two hours later, the senior vice president of leasing emailed back with the precise sales figures for each restaurant. I looked at them, and they were all doing about $1,000 a square foot a year. Now, $1,000 a square foot is spectacular—the gold standard for restaurant operations. In our entire portfolio, we had only a couple of restaurants doing more than that. Naturally, I signed the deal.

With this interesting email exchange in hand, we had a smoking gun. I told the lawyer that in hindsight, no way was any restaurant in that shopping center truly doing $1,000 a square foot in sales at that time. Maybe half that. It was impossible. If we had been given the true sales figures on the other restaurants, I never would have gone forward.

Our attorney told us that if this was true, and the sales figures were actually that far off, then the landlord's information was tantamount to fraudulent inducement, and we had a case.

We drafted a letter to their attorney, asking them to share with us all the sales for each of their restaurants back when we opened in September 2008. The landlord's counsel replied with a long-winded letter telling us that the lease negated all prior discussions and representations. Essentially, they told us to go and pound salt.

We hired a local attorney to co-represent us and make sure all our t's were crossed and our i's were dotted. There was no time to waste. It was now June 2011, and the statute of limitations for a civil fraud claim would run out in September 2011. We prepared all documents for a civil lawsuit to sue the landlord for $20 million—an amount based upon not only our immediate damages in Scottsdale, but also the cost of opportunities lost because our capital had been tied up there. We set a September 12th deadline, after which we would file suit.

The lawyers went back and forth in fruitless exchanges. Then we got a call in early September, inviting us to Los Angeles to meet with the CEO and the legal counsel of the real estate company. Our threat letters and draft complaint had made their way to the top. Clearly, we'd captured their attention. David Miller and I hopped on a plane with our attorney and prepped for the meeting on the way out there.

The negotiations and settlement terms for our exit from Scottsdale are confidential, but I can say this much: when David and I strolled out of the corporate headquarters in LA and jumped into our town car, we looked at each other, smiled, and shared a big high five. Mission accomplished. The bleeding would stop, and we would not be paying millions of dollars to get out of the lease.

It so happened that a team of our chefs was in Orange County that same day researching some restaurants. We met up with them and had a fun night celebrating our victory of having this burden lifted. It made the painful Scottsdale experience so much easier to take. Needless to say, I was thrilled that I had taken the risk and paid that $25,000 to have the lawyer turn over every stone. It was worth every penny.

By the end of 2011, we'd gotten up from the floor. We weren't quite standing, but at least we were sitting up and breathing again. We knew we would survive.

* * *

In late 2011, we opened an Ocean Prime in Atlanta, Georgia, and a year later, we opened our eighth Ocean Prime in Indianapolis, Indiana. They performed moderately well. As 2012 went on, the economy improved and we grew more confident, but out of the corner of my eye, something caught my attention. Sales in Dallas and Tampa, our superstar locations, were starting to leak—nothing dramatic, but I noticed.

One night, I woke up uneasy, thinking about Ocean Prime. I wanted to build a national brand, but I could see the early warning signs, and knew something was not quite right. It felt as if we were driving an eight-cylinder engine with only six cylinders firing properly. The engine just didn't have the right sound. I knew Ocean Prime had good bones, like a house with tall ceilings and a beautiful design foundation, but I also knew we could do better.

I got out of bed at two in the morning and sat at the computer in my shorts until sunrise, studying our competitors and searching my soul. The next morning, I called an executive team meeting to discuss where Ocean Prime was at that moment and where it needed to be. I challenged the team to work on the brand in the coming year. "We need to look at everything: the food, the atmosphere, the décor, the uniforms, the website, the music. And why we are we calling it a modern American supper club?" I asked. "What is that?"

If we didn't do anything, I knew sales would drop, even in our best locations. In order for the brand to be strong for years to come, it needed to be rock-solid and sustainable, growing in sales every year. We needed to have full faith and confidence that we knew everything there was to know about it. All through 2012, we took this journey.

By the end of the year, the most important thing was that we'd survived five grueling years of recession. I was very proud that we had not had any layoffs. I now felt we could face anything. Through difficult times, some of the most difficult of my career, our culture was not only alive and well, it was stronger than ever.

THE BIG RISE

–

2013-2018

In June 2013, I turned fifty. During the months leading up to this moment, I felt a tremendous amount of anxiety about aging. Where had the time gone? More was behind me than in front of me, and I feared the ride was winding down. When my birthday finally arrived, my wife, Molly, threw a beautiful party in our back yard and invited 150 of our friends. She and the kids surprised me with an extraordinary video they'd made for the occasion. It was clever and funny, but best of all, it showed an immense expression of love. Everyone was in tears, including me, and I was filled with gratitude. All my anxieties about aging washed away that night, and I felt more complete than ever before in my life.

I was breathing easier since our company had gotten out of trouble and stabilized, but we were a long, long way from where we needed to be. I knew that in order to repair the damage I had done and create financial security for the future, we would need to dig deep and go for one more major expansion. I yearned to build Ocean Prime into a national brand in order to be completely healed, and I would have to push the company hard and take big risks. In the past, our expansions had been reckless. For the first one, at the turn of the millennium, I'd been young and made rookie mistakes, opening restaurants scatter-shot without understanding branding the company, selecting the sites, and making a realistic plan. In 2008, after our sale to Ruth's Chris, I drove an expansion based on my hubris, and nearly led us to disaster. This time would be different. We weren't going to make those kinds of mistakes again. We had far more knowledge and skill, and therefore we could drive growth more strategically with clear goals in mind. If we ever got into serious trouble, we had some great Ocean Prime restaurants in Tampa, Denver, and Columbus as security. In an emergency, we could unload the brand in a fire sale and use the proceeds to pay our debts. If this happened, it would be a crushing disappointment not to have achieved my business goals, but at least we'd have our specialty restaurants, our catering business, and our Rusty Bucket restaurants moving forward with no debt. It gave me peace of mind to know we had a backup plan so the company would survive, even if it took much longer than I had ever predicted to become a national company.

BRANDING

We began the Ocean Prime rebranding journey in late 2012 and it went on into 2013 and 2014. The rebranding process involves a combination of art and science, and, when done correctly, takes hundreds and hundreds of hours of evaluation over the course of years. Even when you finally nail down what we call brand DNA, the work keeps going, because a brand is like a puzzle—you can always learn more about it. Tastes and styles change over time, and brands must evolve or be left behind.

That was the case with our DNA for Ocean Prime, which we'd launched in 2008 as a "modern American supper club" where "the Rat Pack meets *Sex in the City*." With live piano, big pours, table lamps, and three-page black menu books, we were going for timeless elegance. As we looked at it in 2012 and 2013, we could see this idea wasn't well articulated, and we set out to question all our assumptions about everything, from the décor to the uniforms to the music—and, of course, the food. As we tried out changes, we tested and monitored the results, then continued honing. These were skills I did not understand as a young restaurateur, but learned over time, especially when we changed the décor of our Fish Markets and saw a major increase in profitability.

The first step was research. We interviewed our associates, because they have the most direct contact with guests and know what guests want. We asked them to evaluate everything we were doing and got them involved in the discussions, especially once we started to experiment with changes. We also mined vast amounts of our own data as well as information from Open Table®, the online reservation system that collects ratings and feedback. When we started the project, our average ratings on Open Table® were 89 to 90 percent. We knew empirically that when you float below 90 percent, you start seeing negative sales. We also brought in Andrew Freeman and his nationally-recognized restaurant public relations firm, af&co., to help guide the process. Freeman's group quickly became invaluable to us.

Some changes were obvious. For example, in the original Ocean Prime, we served a vegetable crudité that went out to the table when guests were seated. It seemed like a nice idea in the beginning—a Midwest supper club tradition. The reality was, many guests didn't like it or touch it, and those who did might not order an appetizer as a result. Did we really want our guests to eat a complimentary vegetable crudité instead of ordering our incredible Ocean Prime food? Not to mention the fact that the crudité cost us $200,000 a year and required extra work from our staff. We dropped the crudité because it was doubly negative: it was costing us money without bringing a return, and our guests weren't enthusiastic about it.

Cold blue lights were changed to warm, soft amber. We launched an extensive cocktail program and made the wine list easier to use. The menu went from a bulky three pages to a clean, easy-to-read two. As the brand became more contemporary, Bruno Mars replaced Frank Sinatra, and the piano bar became a lounge.

Based on our research, we understood that the food needed to be lighter. We added a greater variety and depth of seafood, and we made our presentations more minimal. We even reconsidered small details, such as whether to keep using our beloved proprietary seasoning on steaks. We'd always thought this special blend was super cool, but to our surprise, blind taste tests revealed that a majority of people preferred steaks simply seasoned with salt and pepper. We had a similar experience when we eliminated a demi-glace sauce in favor of a simple drizzle of clarified butter over the steak.

Adding sushi was the biggest change of all. Sushi is light and forward-thinking, but our chefs gave us pushback because it was a radical introduction, and they weren't confident they could do it. We trained them and tested the results. The sushi got a great response from our guests, and turned out to be a perfect addition to the menu. We now have a wonderful sushi program at all Ocean Prime locations across the country. It was a great decision.

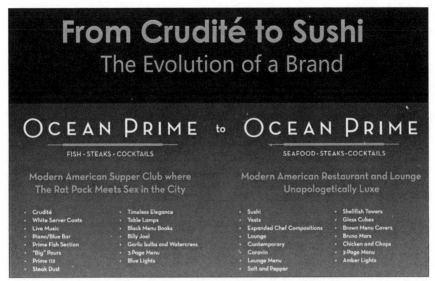

From Crudité to Sushi
The Evolution of a Brand

OCEAN PRIME *to* OCEAN PRIME

FISH · STEAKS · COCKTAILS   SEAFOOD · STEAKS · COCKTAILS

Modern American Supper Club where   Modern American Restaurant and Lounge
The Rat Pack Meets Sex in the City   Unapologetically Luxe

· Crudité	· Timeless Elegance	· Sushi	· Shellfish Towers
· White Server Coats	· Table Lamps	· Vests	· Glass Cubes
· Live Music	· Black Menu Books	· Expanded Chef Compositions	· Brown Menu Covers
· Piano/Blue Bar	· Billy Joel	· Lounge	· Bruno Mars
· Prime Fish Section	· Garlic bulbs and Watercress	· Contemporary	· Chicken and Chops
· "Big" Pours	· 3 Page Menu	· Coravin	· 2 Page Menu
· Prime 112	· Blue Lights	· Lounge Menu	· Amber Lights
· Steak Dust		· Salt and Pepper	

When our national restaurant brand Ocean Prime hit some road bumps,
we did a painstaking brand DNA analysis of the guest experience and
relaunched the restaurants with major changes.

A BIGGER AND BETTER FINANCIAL PARTNER

In order to proceed, we needed a new financial partner. We'd out-
grown our bank in Columbus and asked Piper Jaffray, the financial
house that had managed our Ruth's Chris sale, for help. In 2013, they
introduced us to Fortress Credit Corp., a major bank and investment
firm based in New York City. Fortress did an in-depth investigation
of our finances, poking into every nook and cranny. They extended
us a $35 million credit facility, which consisted of a $23 million loan
and a $12 million line of credit. This was a tremendous boost for
us, and a stamp of credibility. They have been an excellent financial
partner ever since.

With the Fortress deal behind us, we opened a new Ocean Prime
in Philadelphia, Pennsylvania that fall. It was our first city on the East
Coast, and that was great, but to create a national brand, we knew we
needed to be in the big-league markets of New York City and LA.

In the summer of 2013, we began to make that happen, and signed a lease to open Ocean Prime Beverly Hills with a $5 million budget. Around the same time, I was looking at New York City again. We'd been trying to lease a space for nearly two years in Midtown Manhattan, just off Sixth Avenue in the Fifties blocks. This was prime real estate, and many people, including the landlord, figured our Midwestern company was not up to the task. How could a restaurateur from Columbus, Ohio tackle New York City? Back in 2012, the landlord had told us he didn't like our finances. He was concerned that we would start construction and run out of money, so he wanted us to put up a $4 million letter of credit in order to close the deal. We couldn't and wouldn't do that, so we walked away. In late 2013, I learned the place was still sitting empty. I decided to go back and let them know we had closed a substantial credit facility with Fortress.

"If a major New York City bank two blocks away from you was willing to lend us $35 million, then you should feel very comfortable signing a lease with us," I said. "I assure you that the bank did a very substantial investigation of our credit worthiness before they made this commitment."

The landlord spoke to Fortress, and finally said yes. We signed in January 2014.

The lease commitment was terrifying: fifteen years at $100,000 a month, with annual increases of 3 percent. It added up to nearly a $25 million commitment, plus it would cost us more than $7 million to open. We signed the lease at an executive retreat at my condo in Florida, and everyone was excited. We had a celebratory toast. I went along, of course, but I didn't feel like celebrating yet. I knew I was entering a long period of fear and anxiety. It was a huge gamble. Beverly Hills would open in late 2014, and we'd be in New York City in 2015. Ocean Prime would soon be coast to coast. Despite my concerns, I believed that our great company culture would win the day. In addition, we now understood the Ocean Prime brand, thanks to all the work we'd completed. We were well on our way.

In the midst of opening Beverly Hills and planning our entrance to New York, a tremendous opportunity became available in Boston at the South Seaport District, an incredibly hot area. I knew the site would be fantastic. It was one of those "generational locations," which is to say it might not become available again for another forty years.

Our senior team had serious reservations. They were concerned that Beverly Hills had opened way over budget, and the New York City restaurant was in the works. I was determined to go ahead.

When it was time for one last site visit to decide final approval of the deal, I took David Miller, our president and COO, and Wayne Schick, who by now was our senior vice president of procurement and restaurant planning. Our CFO, Diane Smullen, had weighed in and was frightened by the prospect. "Don't let him do it, whatever you do," she said to them before they left. "Your job is to talk him out of it." Those were her marching orders.

That day, the three of us walked around the Boston seaport. The area was clearly exploding, but at this time, it was under construction, and looked like a war zone. There were huge holes in the ground, big earth-moving machines, and piles of gigantic steel beams. At the end of the day, there would be 17 million square feet of retail, office, and living space, and this massive development was growing at break-neck speed. Our location was in the dead center of it all, like being on the corner of Main and Main Street. There was no better location for a restaurant in the entire Seaport District.

"What do you guys think?" I asked.

They were careful with their words. Yes, it was impressive. Yes, they could see it would be incredible. Ultimately, they voted no. They thought we couldn't afford it, and they worried about living through a construction zone for years. It seemed premature.

Through the decades, we'd built our company on consensus and collaboration with our team. There have been only a few times in our history when I have overridden our team's consensus. This was one of them. This location and deal were too good to pass up. They believed we couldn't afford to do it? I told them we couldn't afford *not* to do it.

We went ahead with the deal, but to ease some of their concerns, I negotiated another million dollars of tenant improvements from the landlord. We'd have to pay it out over time in rent, but at least this slightly improved our cash flow.

COAST TO COAST

By the time we opened Beverly Hills in October 2014, we'd gone over the build out budget by $3 million, and the initial response was not strong. Of course, we expected it would get better, but fear began to radiate through me. When we went out to see what was going on, we could tell as soon as we arrived that something was wrong. We felt unwelcome in our own restaurant. Staff morale was low. How could this be?

It quickly became clear that we'd hired the wrong guy as general manager. Because I'd been intimidated by Beverly Hills, we'd filled that all-important leadership position with someone who was not a part of our company, but who knew the local landscape. I'd thought this would be important in a place like Beverly Hills, and because we so had many of our homegrown people on staff, I thought it would be okay. It wasn't. As general manager, this guy was in charge of the entire restaurant, and he actively resisted our culture. We began losing money right away. In 2015, we replaced him with one of our most beloved general managers, Greg Sage, who wanted to live in Beverly Hills. But by the end of the first year, so much damage had been done that we had lost almost $700,000. Within six months of his arrival, Greg turned that restaurant around. The culture was strong again, and the restaurant started to make a profit. It was another lesson that maintaining our culture and values is our number-one job. Once we do that job well, the profits follow.

All through 2015, while we were coping with the initial losses in Beverly Hills, I was conscious that we had openings looming at the end of the year in New York City and then Boston—within six weeks of each other. If these new restaurants didn't do well, we might face disaster. Boston had gone over budget by nearly $1 million, and New York, with its unions and high prices, had gone over by $3 million.

The great news was that Boston opened to immediate success. It was mobbed from the first day, and it has stayed huge ever since. To-day, our Boston restaurant is doing over $13 million a year in sales, and is our number-three restaurant. It turned out to be the right de-cision, as I just knew it would, because we built on a once-in-a-gen-eration location. Thanks to the appeal of the Seaport District, CMR can make on the order of up to $100 million in profit over the next forty years at that site.

New York City proved an entirely different mountain to climb. At our first opening practice dinner, as we were walking to the restaurant, my son Charlie said, "Dad, aren't you excited? We're in Manhattan."

I replied, "I'll be excited a year from now, if we are still here and doing well."

Our first week, we did $110,000 in sales—half of what I expected. I fought the urge to calculate what this would mean in a year if sales did not improve, but of course, I ran the math. The second week, I was mortified when we did only $110,000 again. I remember being at a conference that I attend every year of forty CEOs—essentially a who's who of the restaurant industry—saying to myself, "My God, what have I done?" At that moment, I was plagued by feelings of inadequacy and worry that the restaurant would fail, but I retained my positive outlook for my peers.

Thank goodness, the third week came in at $160,000, the fourth week at $200,000, and the fifth week at $250,000. By the end of December, Ocean Prime New York City was breaking company records, bringing in $360,000 a week. We'd never seen sales like that before. During the first few weeks, when I was on the edge of my chair, to put it mildly, our slow opening had felt anything but ideal. In fact, it was a blessing to open slowly in a huge market like New York. This gave us time to work out the kinks in our operation.

We did see hope during the early days. Our New York City Open Table® reviews were incredible right from the first day. Clearly, Ocean Prime was resonating with our guests. Our rebranding was complete by then, and the payoff was evident. We were packed for business lunch and happy hour. Soon afterward, we had business and hotel diners coming during midweek. The last piece of the puzzle was Saturday nights. We were slow at first, drawing only eighty to a hundred people because we were in the business district. In time, we drew theater crowds and weekend visitors, and that number rose to three hundred. At just under $10 million in our first year, we were short of my initial $12 million goal, but the restaurant was profitable and steadily growing. I knew we would get there. Today, its sales are over $15 million a year.

Naturally, I felt the stress of being more leveraged than we'd ever been. We'd spent almost $25 million building these three restaurants in major urban markets with big-time rents. It was too early to tell whether our big gamble would pay off. However, I was feeling cautiously optimistic that this expansion had been the right decision. There would be no fire sale anytime soon.

SUPPORTING THE NATIONAL BRAND

Now that we were a national brand, we needed to think differently about marketing. We'd always deployed public relations and advertising for our restaurant openings in regional markets using regional firms, but now we needed to go bigger. We continued to work with Andrew Freeman and his San Francisco firm, asking him to consult on my idea of launching an aggressive national advertising campaign with placements in luxury lifestyle magazines. As part of our national expansion, I wanted to promote Ocean Prime in national outlets.

Amid this work one day, he asked if we'd ever thought about doing a public relations campaign, saying it would be much more effective in serving the Ocean Prime brand. Andrew gave the pitch that spending $1 million on public relations would bring more people into our restaurants than spending $2 million on advertising.

I agreed on the spot. I've learned to trust my judgment when dealing with first-rate talent, and Andrew is just that. We added a national PR firm and then local agencies in all our regions. All the agencies were vetted by Andrew and our VP of marketing, Heather Leonard. Our strategy was to create positive PR around Ocean Prime, our other restaurants, and the CMR brand itself on a continual basis, not just for the openings. The public relations firms needed some time to get to know us and our culture in order to build conversations. It took several months to get traction, but then we started seeing wonderful results.

Public relations for service businesses like ours now has a lot do with cutting out the intermediary, getting buzz started through fun events, meeting people where they are, and giving them an experience of the brand. The goals are to create conversations that are personal, engaging, and social, and to get influential people talking about the brand. Because we place such huge value on creativity and the power of our people, we get everyone involved, and push the envelope to try new things. Though there was some resistance at first, everyone got excited about the campaign when it began showing results.

For example, beginning in 2016, Ocean Prime New York started an annual tradition of giving away hot chocolate to coincide with the lighting of the holiday tree at Rockefeller Center. This was a huge hit. We set up a hot-chocolate bar available from 3:30 p.m. to 7:30 p.m., no purchase necessary. People walked in, warmed up, poured their own cups, and garnished them with cayenne, cocoa powder, mini-marshmallows, and peppermint sticks. This put out great word-of-mouth and name awareness—plus it was a good, generous thing to do, and felt right. Hundreds of people walked through our front door.

The following year, on National Oyster Day®, August 5th, Ocean Prime New York hosted an event with our executive chef, Eugenio Reyes; our executive sous chef, Patrick Rodemeyer; and their team, live-shucking Maine Pemaquid oysters in the lounge for just a dollar apiece. This brought in enormous free media and buzz, and people loved it. Here's another example: to build our before-theater dinner business in 2016, we celebrated by sending Ocean Prime diners away with free, branded bags of the signature truffle popcorn we use as a bar snack. Other theatergoers would notice the bags— hopefully, with envy.

We have found that our after-work lounge promotions and events, such as our Thank Goodness It's Summer Fridays, attract millennial professionals to Ocean Prime. They may not yet be able to afford to dine regularly with us, but they enjoy and identify with the brand.

The public relations firms are doing an amazing job for us, and clearly, Andrew's strategy was on target. Three years after our re-branding was completed, and three years into our national PR efforts, we are seeing 8 percent same-restaurant sales growth in the Ocean Prime brand, which is nearly unheard of in our business.

* * *

In 2018, our mission was accomplished. Ocean Prime is a successful national brand, with thriving restaurants in New York and Los Angeles with Chicago under development —the top three urban markets in the nation—and in other major markets such as Boston, Naples, Tampa, Washington, D.C., Dallas, and Denver. We have sixteen Ocean Prime sites in the East, West, North, and South, with combined sales of $145 million a year. The Ocean Prime brand as a whole has experienced remarkable same-store sales increases year over year since 2014.

Our outward profile was one of success. However, our inward profile needed a facelift. Our old, worn offices on 515 Park Street in Columbus had worked well for over fourteen years, but they no longer represented who we were as a company. While celebrating our twenty-fifth anniversary, we moved into beautiful, shining-new corporate offices—with upscale design, attractive work spaces and meeting rooms, and a well-appointed hospitality and break area—that reflected who we are and our status as a national hospitality company. Today I couldn't be happier. I'll always worry about the business; it's part of my nature as an entrepreneur. People in the office may say I'm still as intense as hell. The truth is, my anxiety washes away far more easily these days, and I enjoy a newfound sense of calm and peace.

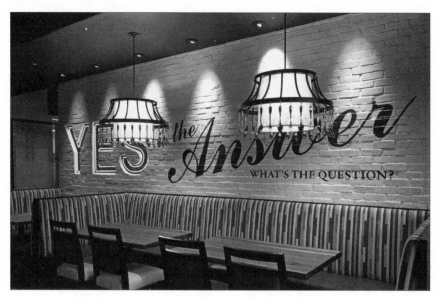

We opened our new corporate offices in 2017, with a design that
honors everything about our culture. This is our lounge and kitchen.
Notice the motto on the wall.

FAITH IN PEOPLE AND A CULTURE OF HOSPITALITY

It's one thing to say that you care about your associates and display inspiring words on your office walls or in your employee manual. It's another thing entirely to instill a positive culture throughout an organization that is meaningful in people's daily work and lives. I've made it clear throughout this book that our culture—our five pillars and eight core values—are the mortar that holds the bricks of the company together. (See them on pages 42-47 if you need a refresher.) The strength of our culture has driven our success for twenty-five years, so I want to share in greater depth how we do it and what it looks like, day in and day out, year after year. In other words, how we walk the talk.

The first step for us is always to make our culture our most important priority. I say that maintaining our culture is job number one for everyone in the company. Job number one(a) is to make a profit—and a damn good profit, so we can build our business, take care of our people, and support our community.

Sometimes, business leaders see a conflict between a positive culture and the drive for profit. For us, there is no conflict. One of our five pillars states that we must "thrive with both cultural and fiscal responsibilities." If there is a choice between the two, the answer is clear: culture wins every time. We never drive profit over culture. In fact, we say that we dedicate 51 percent of our efforts toward maintaining our culture, and 49 percent toward making a profit. If something does not align with our values, we just don't do it. Yet when we compare our bottom-line performance to that of comparable publicly-held companies, we are always at least in the upper quartile, and often the upper 10 percent of profit as a percentage of revenue.

All associates at Cameron Mitchell Restaurants attend a four-hour orientation after they are hired. During the orientation, we take the associates through our culture and values in depth. We also give each of our new associates a copy of our "little red book" and encourage them to carry it for reference. It's a simple brochure that describes our culture's five pillars and eight core values. I am often amazed to see how many of our people, at a moment's notice, can pull out a wrinkled, worn copy of the little red book and share it with pride. Of course, they get a milkshake to reinforce "Yes is the Answer."

In addition to our home office, every restaurant has a group of associates who run the Culture Club for that location. Each year, our Culture Champions oversee the organization of events that celebrate our culture and give associates the opportunity to bond together as a team, sometimes for fun and sometimes for giving back to the community. Examples include Halloween costume parties, Memorial Day cookouts, Thanksgiving dinners for the homeless, shoe and coat drives, chili cook-offs, a taco "throw-down," and many more. Each year, our company ensures that our Culture Champions have the resources to fund these get-togethers.

At orientation, each associate receives our Raving Fan booklet,
which articulates the tenets of our corporate culture.

ASSOCIATES COME FIRST

We put our associates first out of genuine concern for our people, not to manipulate them into working harder or better for us. Our culture puts them first because this is purely how we want to treat them and how we want to value them. In doing so, we attain incredible results.

Our company is built by its people and for its people. Most wake up in the morning feeling they belong to something special. CMR is their home and their family. Associates stay for five, ten, fifteen, twenty, even twenty-five years, as proven by our turnover rates, which are historically well below national restaurant averages. If I've heard it once, I've heard it a thousand times in meetings, at leadership roundtables, and at other events: People feel they're part of a family at CMR and enjoy coming to work. In 2017, we had only 5 percent turnover of management personnel and 48 percent turnover of hourly associates. According to the U.S. Bureau of Labor Statistics, the industry turnover rate is closer to 35 percent for management and 80 percent for hourly associates.

Even when people must move on, they often do so with affection and gratitude. I have received hundreds of letters over the years from associates who have left us to pursue other endeavors, thanking the company and me for providing them a home and great place to work while they were pursuing their goals outside the restaurant industry.

We have so many "associates come first" stories. One of my favorites is about Valerie, our sous chef in Beverly Hills. David Miller and I were making one of our biannual visits to the restaurant for our president's roundtable meeting, when we sit down and talk with groups of associates and individually with each manager. During our meeting, Valerie told me her younger sister back home in Detroit was gravely ill with cancer. Valerie had transferred to Beverly Hills from Detroit to help with the new restaurant. I asked if she was going to spend some time with her sister soon. She said she'd be going there for Thanksgiving. At the time of this conversation, it was August. "Why are you waiting so long?" I asked. She told me she couldn't afford plane tickets, and didn't have vacation time.

"You do now," I said. "The company will pay for your round-trip airfare, and once a month you can combine your weekly two days off with a couple of personal or vacation days. That way, you'll get four days in a row off to go and visit your sister each month, from now through the end of the year. You were already planning on paying for your airfare Thanksgiving week, so that is on you, and the company will take care of the rest."

She was blown away. The best part was that she was able to see her sister many more times before she passed away far too young.

On a different note, I can't resist sharing my "urinal story," which occurred—yes, you guessed it—when I was standing at a urinal in one of our restaurants. Our sous chef, Joe, walked in and stood next to me. Joe is a big, lovable guy who looks like a disheveled teddy bear. I knew he was married with two kids, and since spring break was near, I asked if he had vacation plans for his family.

"We really wanted to go to Disney World with the kids, but we looked into it, and couldn't afford it," he said. "It is so expensive with hotel, airfare, food, park tickets, and spending money."

I told him to go home and tell his family that they'd be going to Disney World. I'd use my Southwest miles and Marriott points to take care of his airfare and hotel.

"After that, you cover the park tickets and spending money."

Joe almost fell over and asked incredulously, "Are you serious?"

"Absolutely," I said.

There are many, many other stories like this about taking care of our people, including: the chef who needed every other weekend off because of child custody (of course, we made this happen); the servers who worked all night on a large party, only to be stiffed (of course, we helped them out); and the funds raised from associates across the country for their fellow associates at Ocean Prime Naples, which was closed for ten days in 2017 after Hurricane Irma (each associate received nearly $800). The list goes on and on. There are countless "associates come first" stories from the past twenty-five years.

BELIEVING IN PEOPLE

Some companies focus a great deal of effort on the prevention of wrongdoing by the one percent of people who are bad or cannot be trusted. For example, employee theft is a major topic of discussion in the restaurant business. I like to say we don't leave a box of steaks by the back door to make thieves of honest people. To eliminate employee pilferage, we have systems in place, such as locking away our steaks and liquor inventory. This doesn't mean we don't believe in our people; we simply remove the chance for temptation to occur.

We always believe in people, so we lead and manage for the 99 percent who are good. We joke that if you meet someone who was fired from Cameron Mitchell Restaurants, you need to pat the person on the back and say, "Good job," because I assure you, they worked hard at it. We believe in second chances. I almost got fired early in my career for poor performance. Thank goodness my boss didn't do it; a few days later, I had the epiphany that sent me into the restaurant business for the rest of my life. I stand on the shoulders of so many who gave me second chances.

We never regretted giving Michael Ho a second chance. He was hired as an executive chef at Molly Woo's, but he went through a period of challenging personal problems, and his performance suffered. Michael expected to be fired, but that never happened. Brian Hinshaw, our senior vice president of food and beverage, coached Michael through a six-month sabbatical until he straightened out his situation and renewed his identity as a chef. Now Michael is a superstar executive chef at The Barn and well on his way to becoming a regional corporate chef. To this day, he says, "I began to give up on myself and the company, but the company never gave up on me."

Ryan Valentine is currently our director of beverage. Back when he was general manager at one of our restaurants, one of his servers consistently arrived late for her shifts. At first, Ryan wanted to fire her, but we spoke about it, and I asked, "How does she do the rest of her job?"

Ryan hesitated. "Very well," he replied.

It turned out she was one of his top performers but had child-care issues, which she soon resolved. Ryan will tell you how glad he was to give her a second chance.

We truly want all our people to succeed, no matter what position they hold in the company. We have helped to turn so many people's lives around. I always tell people that we are in the success business, not the failure business.

Humans make mistakes. If I fired people for making mistakes, I'd be the first person to go. No one in our company has made bigger mistakes than me. I hold the title. What's most important, though, is how we respond once mistakes have happened. We train our people to follow the three As: Acknowledge, Apologize and Act. Whenever we make mistakes, which we all do on occasion, we respond genuinely with the three As. Almost every guest understands that we care, and finds a way to forgive us. It is the same with our people. They understand that sometimes we are not perfect, and we make mistakes. If we respond with care, concern, and the three As, our people forgive us, too. This creates a foundation of trust in our organization.

DEBUNKING THE MYTHS ABOUT RESTAURANT WORK

Many people believe that when you choose a career in the restaurant business, you are entering a career of long hours, low pay, and a poor quality of life. At CMR, we could not disagree more. We are truly invested in our associates' well-being, not only at work, but also at home. We believe you cannot be successful at work if you are not successful at home, and if you cannot be successful at home, you cannot be successful at work. We believe these two realms are incredibly intertwined. Here are some of the ways we promote our associates' well-being and work-life balance.

I never wanted to work on Christmas, so why would I ask our associates to do so? We are closed for seven major holidays each year, plus Super Bowl Sunday. These days are a time for family, friends, and relaxation. I don't understand why some companies feel they need to be open 365 days a year. I think we can still do well being open only 357 days and closed for those eight days.

A manager who is with CMR for five years is entitled to three weeks of paid vacation and three personal days. Those who are with us for twenty years are entitled to five weeks of paid vacation and five personal days. In total, they have thirty-eight days, or about eight weeks, off each year. When I was going up the ladder, I remember how antsy I felt going on vacation—as if I might be fired or criticized for some unknown reason when I returned. So many people have that feeling, because bosses don't make it clear that you're entitled to vacation and should enjoy it and benefit from the relaxation. I make sure to encourage people to have a good time on their vacation, and feel confident that they can leave work behind and come back refreshed and recharged.

One of my favorite lines is: "You will never make it to all of your kids' events." Even so, I insist, and we practice, using the rest of the phrase: "…but you will make it to more games and events than you'll miss." We want you to see your kid perform in the recital or play in the soccer tournament—whatever the case may be—every chance you can.

We never want associates to quit without giving notice, so why would we quit them without extending the same courtesy? When we close a restaurant, and we have closed a few, we give all associates three weeks notice. Any associate who stays through the closure process gets an additional three weeks severance. We share stories, hugs, and tears, and many of them thank us for being a class act all the way to the end. This stands in stark contrast to the common industry practice of letting associates arrive to a padlocked door with a sign, only to find that their workplace has closed with no notice, no severance, and no communication. That absolutely appalls me. It is just plain wrong. This is a case in point that integrity takes years to build and days to ruin.

When we close a restaurant temporarily for renovation, the process can take anywhere from two weeks to two months. We communicate our plans, and of course, our associates are paid until we reopen. Servers make lower hourly wages than other associates, but they almost always make up for the shortfall on the other end, because the reopening spurs a wave of new business.

We create pathways for upward mobility, filling 80 percent of our management positions by promoting from within. This gives our associates the opportunity to double, triple, and even quadruple their salary as they rise through the company ranks. I always tell our people that all they have to do is look to their right or left, and they'll see an example of someone who is building a career with the company. We want everyone to know that the more they put in, the more they will get out. The culture of our company unshackles people from traditional norms. Once they believe they are truly cared for, respected, and empowered, and know they can go as far as they want, they are essentially hitching their wagon to our horse. I describe this phenomenon as an atmosphere of *intrapreneurship*. The results are spectacular, and the sky is the limit.

Because we look at associates as individuals and reward them based upon merit, we do not follow the typical industry practice of paying bonuses. All too often, bonuses incentivize people to take shortcuts in order to meet their numbers. I believe the bonus system in the restaurant industry is wrong for associates, management, and guests. Bonuses can lead staff into cutting corners, which hurts quality. They can tempt managers into manipulating numbers, which undermines the restaurant overall. For associates, bonuses change the mind-set from doing a great job overall to working for a narrow goal, no matter how it affects other aspects of the restaurant or their own performance.

I believe people want to perform well at work for three reasons: First, they take satisfaction in doing a good job; second, they enjoy being recognized by others for their performance; and third, they want to get promoted and make more money. They don't need a bonus to accomplish any of these goals. We give raises and promotions based upon high-quality individual performance across a full spectrum of activities. Part of putting our people first means that we need to have strong business practices, such as the human resources policies, systems, and procedures that cause us to hold ourselves to a high level of professional performance.

COMMUNICATION AND INFORMATION-SHARING

One of our core values is that we share open, honest communication. The reason is that I believe 95 percent of problems in the restaurant business are due to lack of communication. We make it a point to be in constant contact and communication, and we share information in many ways.

We have a 1-800 hotline that anybody can use to call in with a concern or suggestion. We also create frequent in-person opportunities for communication. The general manager of each restaurant holds a cabinet meeting every three months, at which he or she has a representative from every associate department—for example, a server, a bartender, a cook, and a dishwasher. This meeting gives the associates a chance to sit and talk about what's going on at their restaurant, share information, and resolve problems.

We also require daily pre-shift pit-stop meetings, where managers talk with associates about living out the culture on the floor of the restaurant and sharing additional information, expectations, and concerns of the day.

We want to hear what our associates think. If there is severe weather, we always manage by collaboration and make decisions as a team, allowing people to weigh in about whether we should close or have limited hours. We do the same thing if the electricity goes down or any other problem impacts everyone at a given location. Our communication is constant. I don't think our people feel disconnected at any time whatsoever.

We have two fall and spring meetings that cover three days and two nights, bringing together all our general managers and executive chefs as well as the senior leadership of the company. The spring event is held in Columbus. The fall event is a leadership conference that rotates among three locations. If it's in Columbus this year, it will be in Napa Valley or Sonoma wine country the following year. Every third year, it travels. In 2019, for example, we'll be in Chicago, because we just opened an Ocean Prime restaurant there and we want our managers and senior leadership to experience our Chicago restaurant.

We also hold an annual meeting that lasts three days and two nights, bringing together all assistant managers in the company. This event is also held in Columbus. I find this meeting to be one of the most rewarding and enjoyable of the year, because these are, by and large, our younger associates, who are newer to our culture and are getting the opportunity to talk with leadership. They have wonderful energy and enthusiasm, and give us many opportunities for teaching the CMR way.

One of my favorite events each year is when Molly and I open our doors for a holiday party for our home office team and operating partners from around the country. We fly them in for the night, and they come to our house for a first-class party. Everybody is dressed in their best, and we celebrate into the wee hours of the morning. We really roll out the red carpet, right down to swag gift bags at the end of the night. It is a blast. We started this tradition five years ago, and have no intention of stopping.

In addition to bringing our managers and assistants to us, we go to them with many on-site visits and meetings. Members of our human resources, facilities, and accounting teams visit each restaurant once or twice a year to hold a series of support meetings. We review our business practices, check the files, and ensure that everyone is doing things the way they're supposed to be done.

Because we have many locations across the country, it's especially important that we share a seamless set of companywide business practices that are taught and used properly. We don't really differentiate between a restaurant in Beverly Hills and a restaurant in Tampa. They are all part of the network. We work hard to maintain uniform systems, policies, and procedures. This is simply the framework required to run a national restaurant company.

Twice a year, we have a president's roundtable. David and I visit each of the out-of-town restaurants, sit down, and break bread with a group of associates representing their respective teams. We deliver a State of the Union-type address about what's happening with the company, and then we talk about the individual restaurant's business. We also talk individually with all the managers of that site. We do the same thing with our in-town restaurants and home office team.

Each of the four divisions of our company has its own director of operations and corporate executive chef. The corporate executive chef of the brand and director of operations make it their business to know everything that is going on with that brand, and visit those restaurants all the time.

We also divide our restaurants regionally. We pair regional directors and regional chefs into teams that oversee five or six restaurants. Just as I did when I had five or six restaurants, they make it their business to know their managers well and understand their needs and desires. Each regional director's job is to know the ins and outs of all operations at those five or six restaurants, down to knowing the names of every associate.

Every other week, each member of our ten-person executive team prepares a one- or two-page report about what's going on in his or her world and sends it to every other executive team member. On the opposite weeks, all the regional directors and regional chefs submit a one- or two-page report about what's happening in their restaurants and send it to all members of the executive team as well as all members of their operations team. We all read those reports every week to keep abreast of what's happening in our restaurants across the country. I try to respond to every single one with at least a few words, whether it's "Hey, thanks!" or "Great job!" I do this because I want people to know that I read their reports. If I have issues or other things to discuss with them, I say, "Please see me at your convenience. I've got a couple of items in here I want to discuss further." It is a remarkable way to keep everybody in communication.

We also communicate through other means, such as frequent internal posters to share news about fun things we're doing, exciting things in the company, and stories of raving fans. To express our appreciation, we send individualized cards to associates who get a promotion or reach a milestone, such as a five-, ten-, fifteen-, twenty-, or twenty-five-year work anniversary, personally signed by the executive team to congratulate and celebrate them. Each month, I receive a stack of these cards to sign, and though it is time-consuming, I always take a moment to write something personal and express my thanks.

MEASURING QUALITY

Feedback is the breakfast of champions, which is why we measure everything in our company—from guest counts and sanitation scores, to sales and net income, and everything in between. In addition to soliciting feedback constantly, we generate daily sales reports for each restaurant, along with relevant comparison data—for example, how that restaurant performed the previous year or month.

Some of our most important metrics come from our associate opinion survey, or AOS, which we administer each winter and summer. The survey is voluntary, and is usually completed by more than 97 percent of our associates. All our company managers and leaders, including me, are evaluated. We have been doing this survey from almost the beginning. The survey measures how our culture and values are influencing the company and how much they are resonating within.

In eleven questions, all respondents are asked for feedback on a range of points, such as whether they are proud to work at their restaurant, if they receive the proper tools to do their job, whether the food is of consistent quality, and if the restaurant is clean and well-maintained. We also ask if their restaurant exhibits CMR culture and philosophies, whether they feel they have a voice, and how well the management team works together, provides information, and trains staff.

The survey provides insights for our managers about how they perform and how our people perceive them. This feedback has proven, time and time again, to be invaluable to our continued growth and success. Today the survey results fill a six-inch binder, now approaching three hundred-plus pages of information. We are always comparing our results to prior years and looking for trends. If our goal is to be better today than we were yesterday, and better tomorrow than we are today, we want proof that we are succeeding. I am happy to say we usually achieve the goal, and our survey results rate our cultural impact at 93 percent or 94 percent, year in and year out.

While good scores are wonderful, the survey always shows us where we need to improve. I often meet with the manager who got the worst score in the company and say, "This could be the best day of your life." Then I share my own experience from when I was a young man and nearly had a mutiny on my team. Sometimes, the most painful feedback is the most valuable.

ENCOURAGING PEOPLE TO DREAM

Recently we had a conference with our general managers and chefs, and to celebrate our twenty-fifth anniversary, we staged a dinner at Cameron's of Worthington, which was our very first restaurant. We closed it to guests for a night and had dinner there, and I sat at a table with some young managers. A twenty-five-year-old woman, who had just been promoted to general manager at one of our restaurants, sat next to me, and I learned she was a graduate of the Ohio State University Hospitality Management School.

I like to encourage young people to dream big, think big, and challenge themselves with *what if* questions. I told her that when I'd opened this restaurant twenty-five years earlier, I never would have dreamed that I could be sitting at this conference after having built nearly one hundred restaurants. Now here we were with this incredible company, celebrating twenty-five years.

"Just think," I said. "Over the next twenty-five years, if we build, on average, five or six restaurants a year, we could have two hundred or more restaurants across the country, perhaps internationally, and maybe reach $1.5 billion or even $2 billion in sales."

"And maybe you'll be at this table with some other young twenty-something and saying, 'I remember sitting here with Cameron Mitchell twenty-five years ago for ten minutes. I'll never forget it—he told me I might be here twenty-five years from now, leading a big division of our company. And now here we are, and it has happened.'"

It's vital for me to pass on a legacy of inspiration and motivation for our people, helping them to have faith in themselves and others. During the past twenty-five years, we've changed a lot of people's lives for the better, and that's exciting for me. We are so much more than just a business.

10

2019 AND BEYOND:
LEGACY AND GIVING BACK

On our twenty-fifth anniversary, I am in the fourth quarter of my career, as they say. I have a yellow pad on my desk with a list of goals for this phase of my life. I plan to take more of a stewardship role as chairman of the company. As we head into the next twenty-five years, I want to be confident that we enrich, invest in, and protect our most important assets—which are, of course, our culture, our values, and our great people. In addition, I want to make sure that we enhance the wonderful business we've built and the reputation we've gained for quality and genuine hospitality. These thoughts are at the forefront of my mind as I look ahead.

I am extraordinarily grateful for the contributions and talents of our wonderful associates, who work and live within the values of our company. They have helped us build a culture that has become a living, fluid force in the company—something like a modern-day oracle. If we are confused or need direction, the five pillars and eight core values guide us to ask the right questions: *Is this decision best for the team as a whole?* or *Would this decision put associates first?* or *What does this have to do with being better today than we were yesterday, and better tomorrow than we are today?* These questions always give us clarity.

One of our values has always been that we are committed to the overall growth of the company and the individual growth of our people. You can't have one without another. Learning and growing should last a lifetime.

DEVELOPING THE NEXT GENERATION

The company and I are deeply committed to the education and development of future generations of young people who want to go into the restaurant and hospitality business. Over the years, I've given substantial time and support to the Culinary Institute of America because of my deep love for the school that gave me the strong foundation to build my career. I served on the board as the first alumni chairman—I am now chairman emeritus —and have had wonderful experiences volunteering and fundraising. Best of all, my involvement with the CIA has given me the chance to address and advise hundreds of students and to offer internships and jobs to graduates.

As we move ahead after twenty-five years, I also want to give locally. I'm proud that we have joined with Dr. David Harrison, President of Columbus State Community College, in a major effort to expand the hospitality management program of the school, which currently serves about five hundred students, who are confined to classrooms and kitchens in the dilapidated basement of a very old building. Together we've created a vision for a new Hospitality Management School at Columbus State, featuring a glorious new $33 million building and vastly expanded learning opportunities, which will more than double the school's capacity to over one thousand students.

To help get the job done, Dr. Harrison gathered Columbus's most prominent hospitality business leaders into a group nicknamed the Kitchen Cabinet. The total cost of the project will be $40 million, and the funding will come from many sources. The college has contributed $13 million through a bond offering, the state of Ohio has committed $10 million, and the city of Columbus has pledged $7 million for the beautification of Cleveland Avenue, which borders the front door of the school. To raise the remaining $10 million, we need private funds, and Dr. Harrison asked David Miller and me to co-chair the fundraising committee and lead the charge. Because of my years of philanthropic service and board work at the CIA, I felt prepared to take on this massive capital campaign with confidence that we could get it done. CMR became the lead donor with a gift of $2.5 million.

I am thrilled that our company could make this major gift. Here are my top three reasons why:

1. My love of the Columbus community, which has been so generous in support of our company.

2. My unwavering commitment to the hospitality industry, which has been so good to me, my family, and our people. I will forever be in its debt.

3. My interest in workforce development. As we continue to grow and build restaurants across the country, a state-of-the-art hospitality management school in Columbus will help ensure there is a pipeline of well-trained graduates to join our company, and others, in the food service industry.

For Cameron Mitchell Restaurants, Columbus State is far more than a provider of associate's degrees and the school where I picked up the courses I needed to get into the CIA. Columbus State has twenty-seven thousand students, and is marbled into our company's human development. Hundreds of our associates graduated from or attended Columbus State. More than forty of our company's three hundred-plus managers graduated from this school, including three of our executive team members. Our entire company benefits from the school's excellent education and training.

I was deeply moved when the school announced that the new building would be named Columbus State Hospitality Management School at Mitchell Hall. This learning and community hub is among the first of its kind in the country to be funded by a public-private partnership, and certainly the first of its kind in our region.

Mitchell Hall will be a three-story, 80,000-square-foot building with a four-hundred-seat event/conference center; a professionally managed, student-staffed restaurant and bar; a retail café and bakery with outdoor seating; a hundred-seat culinary theater; seven state-of-the-art teaching and innovation kitchens; a beverage laboratory; farm-to-table gardens; many new classrooms; and a balcony overlooking downtown Columbus. The new building also will offer classes for foodies, events with guest speakers, and all manner of public involvement and community-building.

The expansion of Columbus State Community College's culinary degree program will be a force multiplier for Columbus's food and restaurant industries while generating new opportunities for restaurant professionals of the future. This is the rendering of the new Mitchell Hall that will anchor the program when it opens in 2019.

INVESTING IN THE NEXT GENERATION OF LEADERS

As we move forward, the company and I will invest more time and energy into growing our Young Leaders initiative. In this program, we hand-select fifteen to twenty promising managers each year, giving them opportunities to collaborate with and get to know the executive leadership team by working with them on strategic projects. For example, this year, we have a Young Leadership group of eighteen managers broken into three groups. Two groups are working with the senior leadership team on a new project called the Budd Dairy Food Hall. The other team is working on the design, budgeting, and menus for our new California cuisine restaurant opening in 2019, tentatively named The Del Mar, in Columbus's Short North area. Involvement with the birth and growth of a restaurant provides invaluable learning and experience for these young people.

We created this intergenerational program because our company now has more than three hundred managers, and it's impossible for the senior executive team and me to work closely with them or even get to know them all. Yet in a few years, the Young Leaders will rise in rank and shape the future of our company.

Our goal is that our senior leadership will get to know every single one of these young professionals by name, learn their strengths and interests, and build relationships with them. Conversely, I want the Young Leaders to get to know us. This re-creates the positive chemistry of what happened in the early days of the company, when I had a few restaurants and knew all the associates by name. For years, our offices were housed in our restaurants, and I was constantly in our restaurants, working closely with our staff. I coached young managers and gave them opportunities to learn, grow, and sometimes leap before they felt ready—though I knew they were.

I'm not as intimately involved with the Young Leaders program as some of our other executive team members, but each one of these groups spends a few hours with me on a Saturday afternoon and gets to pick my brain. We don't have an agenda; I just encourage them to talk so we can connect. I enjoy it immensely. During these sessions I like to challenge our Young Leaders to think big and imagine what the future would be like for them in a senior position at CMR. They like to hear the old war stories. We break bread together, and everyone leaves the room with a sense of connection. I always get as much out of it as they do, if not more.

OUR COMMUNITY LEGACY

Someone asked me once, "How much money do you want to make?"

"As much as humanly possible," I replied. I got a strange look, and I could tell the person thought this comment was shallow of me.

"Why would you want to do that? What motivates you?"

"The answer is simple," I said. "The more I make, the more I can give away."

With resources, I have been able to make an impact and help those less fortunate. The classic adage of philanthropy is that you can give time, talent, and treasure. Time, I don't have. My talents are limited. That leaves me to give treasure.

How much fun is it to give away money to help other people and make an impact on your community? I eagerly anticipate having more time to support community organizations that are bringing great talent and solutions to help those in need. As a company, CMR has given several million dollars to charities during the past quarter-century, and will continue doing so long after I am in that big restaurant in the sky.

One of my favorite examples is our support of SON (Serving our Neighbors) Ministries, which helps low-income and immigrant parents in the suburbs to learn English as a second language and access other services for themselves and their children, including job training, summer child care, and lunch programs. The organization is run by my friend, Kim Emch, who is making a huge impact on hundreds of lives by helping families get out of poverty, with a budget of about $500,000 a year. She is an amazing person with incredible drive and energy. When I was first introduced to her, she invited me to a summer event where the kids in the program invited community members to their "café" and served us lunch. I was blown away by what I saw that day. Kim has big aspirations to grow the program, and we will continue to help her and others like her who are making a difference.

Another of my favorite ways we're giving back is our support of the regional KIPP (Knowledge Is Power Program) school. I am on the board with other community leaders in Columbus. This two-thousand-student, K-12 school is led by an amazing executive director, Hannah Powell.

KIPP students are predominantly low-income or impoverished, and the vast majority arrive at school severely behind academically. At KIPP, they receive great teaching, high expectations, and an extended day schedule that provides an enriching haven into the evening hours. Through the generous financial support of Abigail and Les Wexner, and many other great philanthropists, community partners, and businesspeople, KIPP Columbus created its own campus with state-of-the-art facilities. KIPP began in Columbus in 2008, and now we see students graduating from high school with test scores comparable to the best suburban schools in the state. To put it simply, KIPP Columbus is taking two thousand local, underprivileged kids and changing the trajectory of their lives. And with even more students on the waiting list, there are more success stories to come.

A RISING TIDE LIFTS ALL BOATS

Columbus has a strong community of eager, energetic entrepreneurs making their start with food trucks and pop-up restaurants. That's why we developed a social enterprise venture called the Budd Dairy Food Hall, which will license eight to ten spaces to local *foodpreneurs* who are looking to grow. Whether it's a handmade ramen-noodle shop, a tuna poke café, or an artisan bakery, Budd Dairy is just the spot to gain the advantages of being a business within a business.

Budd Dairy will open in 2019, riding the popular food hall trend in cities around the country. It will bring together local artisan food businesses, entertainment, and community. These social enterprises will draw millennials, couples, young families, and foodies to sample the startup cuisine and creative atmosphere. Budd Dairy also will feature a beer garden, live music, and a rooftop bar overlooking the city.

It is a fun project, and yes, we're doing it for profit. But like the rest of our business, profit is not the only motivation. I have an affinity for young people starting out with nothing and trying to make their way. The Budd Dairy Food Hall and the resources of CMR will bring budding food entrepreneurs in from the cold, so to speak, and help them launch businesses by giving them space, access to marketing, and business guidance, if they wish.

Because we have only eight to ten spots to lease, the selection process is competitive. Final-round applicants come to our office to audition their wares and discuss their ideas. Recently, I was talking with a group of young guys who had just fed us lunch when one said, "We normally would be out in the truck today, but we came here, instead." I was saddened by that, thinking, *My goodness, these guys don't have a lot of money, and they can't afford to lose a day's revenue.* So I asked Steve Weis, our vice president of development who is also in charge of the food hall project, to give $250 in cash and $250 in our restaurant gift certificates (or commensurate compensation) to each group that misses a day's work and uses their own limited resources so they can try out for Budd Dairy Food Hall.

Our family at CMR has immensely enjoyed recruiting, meeting, and tasting the creations of Columbus's up-and-coming chefs who will be part of Columbus's first restaurant incubator, Budd Dairy Food Hall. Budd Dairy will offer a dynamic social hub for experiencing a top culinary creations, a beer garden, and a rooftop deck where people can gather.

If all goes well in the food hall, it will be a great financial success for us. Even more importantly, we expect to see one or two of the superstars coming out of this incubator move to the next level, into brick-and-mortar restaurants. A distant secondary goal, if we allow ourselves to dream a little, would be to partner with these young ventures and provide capital, marketing, construction, or human resources support to help them succeed on a larger scale.

When I was younger, I worried about competition. I've changed now, and I see clearly that a rising tide lifts all boats. Plus, I continue to believe that the more you give, the more you receive. I take great pride in helping young entrepreneurs flourish and thrive.

THE STEWARDSHIP LEGACY

One of the biggest cornerstones of our legacy and values is ensuring we are equipped to take care of our people. I want to know that the people who help build and work in this company for twenty or thirty years will be well rewarded financially, intellectually, and emotionally so they can look back at their career with fondness and pride. I want them to say, "I've got a very nice retirement plan, and the company has been very good to me. I feel happy and fulfilled in my career."

While the success of a restaurant company called Cameron Mitchell Restaurants can be debated, one thing that cannot be questioned is the sense of family that we have created, and our associates have enjoyed. I hear it all the time when I am traveling among our restaurants: "This isn't a job. It's a family." To me, this is one of our greatest accomplishments, and we'll be sure this legacy never changes. Not only are we a family; we build families. We've had dozens and dozens, if not hundreds, of CMR marriages among associates, and even more CMR babies.

A few months ago, I happened to be at one of our Detroit restaurants when the dishwasher mentioned that he and his girlfriend, one of our prep chefs, would be visiting Columbus. I told them to come to the home office and say hello. Sure enough, they showed up, and I gave them a tour of the corporate headquarters. Before we said goodbye, I gave them a $100 gift certificate to use at any of our restaurants anytime. This is genuine hospitality, the way I would treat my own family. I have no intention of gain. It's my pleasure, and runs to the depths of my heart.

As I move to a chairman's position and stewardship role in the future, I will find ways to stay connected to our people and the creative development of our business. Stewardship means guiding and leading. Amid many years of the frenzy and intensity of building restaurants, I haven't always been able to do this. I look forward to connecting with our people in new ways.

No doubt, I will face challenges in taking a step back. I've been thriving on nonstop intensity for twenty-five years, but I trust our team ten thousand percent. I am looking forward to my new role and the next phase of life in keeping our culture strong, continuing to help others, giving back to the community, and enjoying the fruits of my labor.

As a part of my legacy, I have thoughtfully and intentionally transitioned away from doing day-to-day business. One of the great definitions of leadership is being able to let go and pass on the torch. My transition creates a transition all the way down the line.

After almost twenty-five years, my marriage with Molly is strong, and our kids soon will transition into adulthood. Molly and I love to travel and explore, and we will spend more time together, taking adventures. We have so much to anticipate and enjoy.

THE STATE OF OUR COMPANY IS STRONG

I wouldn't be writing these words if I didn't think our company was in good shape. We've worked hard in our first twenty-five years, through ups and downs and mistakes. We've learned. And yes, we have built great restaurants around the country, some in trophy locations that will be there for the next thirty or forty years. In addition, we have an incredible company culture and values. We will always be better today than yesterday, and better tomorrow than today. We will always continue to develop new concepts and spread our wings. Creativity is part of who we are.

We are fortunate to have reached the point where we do not have to go out and raise capital from investors. The company enjoys a strong level of profitability. In fact, we'll never have to borrow another dollar to build more restaurants in the future. We can do it from our own cash flow, while paying dividends to our investors as well as paying principal and interest on our debts. We've reached the point of self-sufficiency. The risk has paid off.

I know that the coming years will hold bust and boom times, and I believe we are in the position to weather a downturn. We don't have to grow if we don't want to, because we have built a company that is going to sustain us. We can open three or four restaurants a year, or one or two—it's up to us. We know we don't need to take the kinds of risks that we did in the past, when we sometimes ended up with self-inflicted wounds.

I'll never forget the joy and the pain we experienced during the last twenty-five years, and I will never, ever over expand again. Let me shout that out from the mountaintops. It won't happen here again. We will never get to a point where the stress is out of control.

As I sit in this beautiful office, looking at downtown Columbus, my family photographs, and our awards, I regret my mistakes, but I wouldn't change a thing, any more than I would change what I learned becoming a runaway or dropping out of school. Those were our experiences and choices, and we have arrived on higher ground. They have made us who we are now.

On our twenty-fifth anniversary, we have a lot of extraordinary work by many extraordinary people to celebrate. I can't imagine anyone who looks forward to coming to work more than I do, and the biggest reason is our people. Now is a wonderful time. We've paid our dues. We've paid our ticket to take our place in the front row of life. We can look out from our restaurants and enjoy the vast and wonderful diversity and spectacle of life in America.

I will never forget all the amazing people who stood with me and by me on any particular day of this wonderful life. First and foremost are my wife, Molly, and our children: Charlie, Ross, and Louise. In addition to them, there are the five groups we always want to be our raving fans: our fellow associates, our guests, our purveyors, our partners, and the communities in which we serve and do business. Finally, to the thousands of people who helped me along the way: I can't thank you enough. I hope every reader who picks up this book will take to heart our message: *Yes is the answer. What is the question?* Look at how powerful faith in people can be.

IN MEMORIAM

I can't write a book about Cameron Mitchell Restaurants and our history and success without writing about my dear friend, Michael Bloch, who passed away in May 2016 at the age of seventy-nine.

I met Michael before starting Cameron Mitchell Restaurants. He was the founder of Michael's Finer Meats and Seafoods in Columbus. I had purchased meat from Michael's for years at my two previous companies before starting CMR. Back then, I said, "I want to be like Mike!" He was successful, well established in the Columbus community, a great businessman, a great family man, and a great all-around guy. Michael was genuinely liked by all who knew him.

For me, Michael was and always will be the most influential man in my life. When I started my business, I went to Michael and asked him if he would extend me thirty days' credit to help me get started. He was not one to extend credit easily, but in my case, he said, "Absolutely!" I started buying from Michael's on thirty days' credit on day one, and I like to joke that I have been on forty-five days' credit ever since!

Michael and I ran into each other at his golf club one day a couple of years after I started the business. We sat down and enjoyed a few drinks together. That was the beginning of a long friendship. Michael and I had every relationship you could have. He was my surrogate father, my mentor, my friend, my partner, my purveyor, my golfing buddy, my gambling buddy, and sometimes, my banking buddy.

Michael Bloch and me at the opening of Mitchell's Steakhouse, 1998.

One day in early 1999, I was trying to buy a building and piece of land at Crosswoods in Columbus to build a second Mitchell's Steakhouse. I had agreed to a contract for $1,725,000, put down a non-refundable deposit of $75,000, and needed $1,650,000 to close. It was the Wednesday before we were supposed to close, and I couldn't get traditional financing. I had to strike a deal with a firm out of Detroit (which I would say was ominous, at best, but it was all I could do). By chance, Michael called me on the phone that Wednesday to "chit-chat," as he liked to say. He casually asked how my deal was going for the new steakhouse. I told him about my problems, and he paused for a minute, then said, "Here is what I would like you to do. Hang up the phone and call that guy in Detroit and tell him to go f*#k himself. I will lend you the $1,650,000 at my borrowing rate, interest only, for two years. You cover my interest costs and pay me back at the end of the two years."

That was the kind of guy Michael was. He lent me millions of dollars over the years when I needed it. He could be tough on me sometimes, but he would always give me a hug afterwards. I never, ever bought from another meat purveyor. Michael was my confidant. I have emulated Michael all my life. To this very day, I still wish to "be like Mike!" Michael, I will always miss you, my friend.

Thank you for all you did for me, and especially for being the most influential man in my life. I will forever and always be grateful to have known you.

ACKNOWLEDGEMENTS

I have been blessed with the support of thousands of people who have all, in one way or another, helped push and encourage Cameron Mitchell Restaurants to keep moving forward all these years. It is impossible to list everyone, but to all of you who have had a hand in our success, I simply say, "Thank you." I am forever grateful. There are a few people I would like to highlight here and now.

First, thank you to my wife, Molly, and our children: Charlie, Ross, and Louise. Thank you for your support, understanding, and patience with me all these years. You are truly the light of my life, and I love you all so much.

Our family in 2016: Molly, Ross, me, Louise, and Charlie. *Photo by Anne Ciotola Photography.*

I also would like to thank our executive team. Without your leadership, guidance, support, tremendous talent, and hard work over the years, we never would have gotten here.

David Miller, President and COO – David has worked alongside me for almost our entire company history. He works tirelessly. Our company is in good hands with David as our president and chief operating officer.

Stacey Connaughton, Vice President of Corporate Affairs – Stacey has faithfully and diligently supported the company and me since day one. It has been a pleasure to work side by side with her all these years.

Diane Smullen, Chief Financial Officer – I have seen Diane get married and have three babies over the years. She is tenacious about being a great CFO, mom, and wife. I am always amazed at how she does it all.

Heather Leonard, Vice President of Marketing – Heather's continued energy and devotion to her team and to our marketing vision and execution, down to the smallest detail, is awesome and inspiring.

Chuck Davis, Vice President, Human Resources – Chuck is our human resources anchor. I have always said we have a great human resources practice within our company because of Chuck.

Wayne Schick, Sr., Vice President of Procurement & Restaurant Planning – Wayne is one of the smartest guys I know. He continues every day to hone our purchasing programs and design at our restaurants with an incredible attention to detail.

Brian Hinshaw, Sr. Vice President, Food & Beverage – Brian is not only a great guy, but he is the best cook I have ever known. He is a great inspiration to all of our chefs company-wide.

Chuck Kline, Sr. Vice President of Operations – Chuck has a great restaurant mind. I have loved working with Chuck over these past twenty-two years, watching him grow from a young sous chef to se-nior vice president of operations.

Steve Weis, Vice President of Development – Steve is a late addi-tion to our team, four years ago. What a great hire. Steve fits into our organization like a glove.

Gary Callicoat, President, Rusty Bucket Restaurant & Tavern – My almost brother-in-law and longtime dear friend. What a great success story we have built with the Rusty Bucket.

I offer special thanks to our nearly five thousand associates com-pany-wide. I am so proud of all of you. Thank you for all you do for CMR. Thank you for making raving fans and delivering genuine hospitality!

To our guests: Thank you for your continued patronage and sup-port of Cameron Mitchell Restaurants. On behalf of all of us at CMR, thank you for allowing us to be of service to you. We look forward to serving you for many years to come.

To our partners: Without you, we could never have been in busi-ness in the first place. Your continued support and investment in Cameron Mitchell Restaurants have helped us build a tremendous amount of brand equity and a good return on investment. Howev-er, your investment has provided much more than that. You have helped create thousands of jobs and provide rewarding careers for many, many people. Your investment has helped positively impact thousands and thousands of lives over the years. Special thanks to Bob Liebert, Bill Emery, Michael Glimcher, Alan Rudy, and Kent Bowen for their time, advice, and never-ending support.

To our purveyors: You have been our partners in business all these years. Your support of Cameron Mitchell Restaurants has been in-valuable to our success. Your willingness to extend credit terms to us, your incredible service, and your support of our company have been extraordinary. The quality products you provide us have enabled us to deliver that same quality to our guests. It has been a real pleasure to build our businesses together. Thank you.

To our communities: I want to thank the communities in which we do business, especially Columbus, Ohio—hometown to me and Cameron Mitchell Restaurants. Your support has been incredible. We have taken great pride in growing with you along the way. We have been able to give back millions of dollars to countless charities and organizations in Columbus and our other communities, helping others improve their lives. It truly has been a labor of love. Thank you for all your support, and for the opportunity to give back all these years and become part of the fabric of our cities.

I also want to thank my trainer, DaVaun Summers, and my yoga instructor, Laurel Hodory. You two ladies have been instrumental in keeping me on a fitness regimen for both my physical and mental well-being, which is so important, especially in stressful times.

Finally, I would like to thank those who made this book possible. Thank you, Laura Schenone and Herb Schaffner, who helped me write this book. You have spent hundreds and hundreds of hours on my project and put all your incredible talent to work to help me write this book in my voice. You both did a fantastic job, and I thank you. I also want to thank my publisher, Rohit Bhargava of IdeaPress. Thank you for assembling a great team and for trusting in me and taking on this project. We couldn't have done it without you.

APPENDIX
–
RAVING FAN STORIES

The following pages are just a small example of the hundreds of letters we have received from guests, associates, community organizations, and purveyors over the years. They are perfect illustrations of our culture and philosophies in action and their long-lasting impact.

Team Tampa,
What an awesome letter
and what an awesome display
of Genuine Hospitality and making
Raving Fans! I am so proud of
all of you. Great Job!
Sincerely,
Cam

Messrs. Cameron Mitchell and Alex Bates

390 W. Nationwide Blvd.

Columbus, OH 43215

Dear Sirs:

For the past 3 to 4 years I have been a Friday night regular at your Tampa Ocean Prime restaurant. (More or less the Norm at OP). I was told by friends that OP was a great place so my first visit convinced me they were right. Lauren Huttle was my bartender and she made me feel at home, so I knew that my 45 mile trip to Tampa was going to be a regular trip on Friday nights.

Over the past 3 to 4 years, I didn't miss too many Friday nights. In that time I got to know many of the staff and of course some regulars that go there.

Then on 2/1/18, I was diagnosed with stage 4 prostate cancer that had metastasized to my bones, lungs and lymph nodes. I told Lauren and other staff members that I would not be there for awhile and the following Friday night would be that last one for awhile.

The following Friday night I came in Sierra Peretz along with one of the managers Jonathan Pollock gave me a T-Shirt, I have a picture with Sierra and Jonathan enclosed, also one with Lauren. The shirt was signed by some of the members of the staff.

The managers, forgive me if I don't know all the last names, Kal, Jonathan and Valarie Bauer. The hostesses who all give me the greatest smile when I come in (Sierra, Lindsey Jensen, Sara Blom) the bartenders, Lauren, David Lee, Jessica Lea, Ryan Austraw, Jarrett Johnson, Olivia, James, Jeff, Jasem and also some of the servers, Emanuel Martinez, Paige Raza, Justin Egan, Drew, Richard Spears. There are others I'm sure I missed but your staff is the greatest.

I'm an old guy with my son and daughter in Ohio and Virginia so the staff over the years has been so kind to me I look at all of them as my Florida family. They may not realize how important my trips to Tampa were and to see all the smiling faces.

Since I was diagnosed I have not been there regularly but Lauren always hooks me up with ice tea and not my regular Dewars.

I realize that one of these days I will have to go back north to be with my children but I just wanted you to know that your staff at Tampa is great and I will miss them when the time comes.

Thank you!

Respectfully,

Bob Bazzel

Bob

Dear Cameron,

Our son has been at Nationwide Children's Hospital since August 4th. He was diagnosed with severe aplastic anemia which is a rare blood disease that destroys your bone marrow — making it not able to produce any blood cells.

Zac has been craving Orange Chicken since he got in the hospital. We tried to get delivery everywhere and nothing was open until early evening. This was on a Sunday at about noonish. We wanted to find him Orange Chicken since he just got out of a bone marrow procedure and been poked all night with blood draws. So we felt he deserved some Orange Chicken. So his grandpa called Molly Woo's and they said they didn't make it nor do they deliver from Polaris to Nationwide Children's. Then the manager said let me check something and asked if we could call back in five minutes.

When we called back in five minutes, the manager said to us, "My sous chef can make that for your son and he will personally deliver it to you." WOW. We were just amazed at the kindness and gesture. So the sous chef delivered it to Children's Hospital and also had a gift card and said, "This one is on us, we are rooting for ya." Grandpa insisted and threw $40 in his car as he drove away.

But THAT is customer service and care. This is something special we will never forget and we appreciate the entire Molly Woo's team for putting a huge smile on our son's face.

WE WILL BE BACK!!!! Thank you for caring, Molly Woo's!

— Jonathan Wagner

CAMERON MITCHELL RESTAURANTS

November 15, 2017

Cameron Mitchell
Cameron Mitchell Restauran
390 West Nationwide Blvd.
Columbus, OH 43215

Dear Mr. Mitchell,

My partner Scott and I are regular and loyal customers to your restaurants and have continuously had a positive experience. I tell friends and visitors to Columbus that I am "addicted" to your restaurants because of the wonderful food, but mainly because your staff members are absolutely outstanding. Every single time I am in one of your restaurants, I am amazed again and again. This includes two recent visits.

I started a new position at Ohio State on November 1, where I have been employed for 25 years. Scott and I decided we wanted to celebrate, so he made arrangements for a nice dinner at M. Of course, every step of the way, the evening was perfect. Joe Hahn and the entire staff made me feel like I was the only person in the restaurant that night. The dinner was just amazing and we had an incredible experience. Linda took great care of us that night and everyone was great. Please let the team there know that once again, they exceeded our expectations!

The next night, we decided that we would go to The Avenue in Grandview for the Tri-Village Restaurant Week celebration. Scott and I made a reservation for four with our friends Kevin and Shawn. I thought we were just headed to a nice dinner out. The second we walked into the restaurant, Kristen and Korin made it clear that they knew I had accepted a new job at Ohio State and that the celebration was on. We had not said anything, but knowing Kristen and her amazing attention to detail, and knowing the Hahn connection, it was clear that the M staff and the Avenue staff had conspired to ensure that we would have a great night out. We had an amazing meal, finished with a wonderful surprise dessert!

I cannot express how happy both nights made me. You and your team are an important part of the Columbus community all of these years because you pay attention to detail and you are building incredible leaders in your company who serve in manager roles. Leading teams and motivating them in the service industry requires heavy lifting and your restaurant leaders are doing incredibly great work. Please know of my continued happiness with your company and know that Scott and I continue to sing your praises. We are so pleased that you continue to offer such genuine hospitality that is just unparalleled. Thank you for your commitment to Columbus.

Have a wonderful holiday season!

Best wishes,

Donald A. Stenta, PhD
Assistant Vice President, Alumni Experiences
The Ohio State University Alumni Association

received 6-15-10

Cam, David, Stacy & CMR Family—
As I am in my new career 60 days
and blessed to recieve the time and
training to grow my leadership skills,
I realize that it all comes back to my
days at CMR. Thank you for your culture,
Thanks for shining great leadership.
Thanks for teaching empowerment—
"Enlarging others makes you larger."
Every day I am blessed to have the
life I created—with the help and
support of others. Over 10 years ago—
actually, 13, I didn't "get" what was
happening right in front of me working
for you—But now I do, and I
am grateful every day for the opportunity.
So if I haven't said it before, Thank You!
Thanks for the leaders that you are—
I want my office to run on the
same energy. It's amazing the
synergy it creates, and the success that
will come. I wish every one of you all the
Best for a happy & fulfilling future!

Caryn Schmidt

Name *	Mary Shamoon
Email *	████████████
Zip Code *	60062
Phone Number	████████

General Comments/Inquiries

So I want to tell you a story about one of your managers Heather Queen who went above & beyond her job.

My son just moved down to the Dallas area from Chicago for work. He would not be coming home for Easter Dinner. I have been concerned about him eating a decent meal on Easter. With no one down there to invite him to dinner. I was looking for a place to make him a steak as that is his favorite. I was going to surprise him & have it deliverer to his apt. Well, I can tell you that Heather helped me out big time as I was looking for a restaurant that had all his favorites. Not only did I see you served steak but sushi as well. I spoke with Heather a week in advance. I told her I was trying to figure out how I could get the food delivered to my son on Easter. I also fell off the chair when she said they she would deliver it. She said then she knew he would get it & it would be fresh & right. I told her I would pay to have it delivered & flat out refused. She states that she did not live far from where he was at & that it would not be a problem. I cannot tell you how appreciative I was. My son was thrilled when she showed up at the door. She refused any reimbursement even for gas. My son was so excited he called us to show up what he got & then continued to say it was the most tender steak he had ever had. It was cooked perfectly along with Sushi was delicious. Everything was perfect! I am a nurse & do lots of random acts of kindness to help others. I don't think I have ever been on the receiving end of someone going out of there way of such an act of kindness. I cannot tell you how truly grateful I am to Heather for making sure my son had a decent meal after working from 5 in the morning. I feel kind of guilty for putting her out. I just wanted to let you know how lucky you are to have such a person working for you. It not only speaks volumes for her but for your organization and the people you hire. You can bet when we come down to visit my son later in the year. We will be dining at your restaurant.

Best Regards to you ,

With appreciation,

Mary Ann Shamoon

Recvd
4-2-18

Cameron,

I'm sure you are aware by now that at the beginning of March I officially left Cameron Mitchell Restaurants after nearly 7 years with the company. Of course, it is nothing against CMR, just that my time has come to do something different. I am writing to personally thank you for the opportunities I've been given and for everything CMR has done for me. I grew up in the kitchen at Ocean Prime Denver and am extremely proud of everything I've been able to accomplish there. The staff has become my second family and Bill, Roman, and Leo have become my biggest mentors in both career and life. The skills and experience I have gained with this company have prepared me to go into the world with confidence. I'm sure we will meet again, so until then, Thank you again for the knowledge and the opportunity.

- Taylor Kellenaers

From: raymond.s.toroyan < ██████████████████ >

Sent: Monday, September 11, 2017 12:06 PM

To: Cameron Mitchell

Subject: Thank You

Dear Mr. Mitchell

My name is Raymond Toroyan and I am a student at the CIA. I'm about 8 weeks into my externship at Ocean Prime – Troy and learning there has made me realize how great an impact your legacy has had on my career. At every step of the way so far you are, in some way or another, involved in my life as a culinary student.

I got my first job at The Rusty Bucket – Bloomfield Hills while I was starting culinary arts at my high schools VOC program. After high school, I came to learn and work with the best at CIA, where you were on the board of trustees and contribute a great amount in scholarships. Now, I'm doing externship at Ocean Prime. Reflecting back on my past experiences, I realize how grateful I am to have done most of my learning and growing in your restaurants. There is something truly unique about the community you've built. There is a great deal of care, understanding and passion that flows through the walls of your restaurants and associates. Because of that, I know that I wouldn't have learned nearly as much anywhere else.

I wanted to take the time to thank you for all the great opportunities you've afforded me as a student, as well as throughout my career in the culinary arts. Because I truly believe that I wouldn't be where I am today if it weren't for you.

Respectfully,

Raymond Toroyan

-----Original Message-----
From: Rob Snow - SUFD [mailto:rob@standupfordowns.org]
Sent: Thursday, August 04, 2016 3:59 PM
To: Cameron Mitchell; Diane Smullen
Subject: Thank You and Excellent Job!

Hi Diane and Cameron,

Just wanted to shoot you both an email and thank you for allowing us the opportunity to use the Ivory Room for our event last Friday. Truly an amazing space complimented by all of our guests.

Your staff lead by Krystin VanHorn was excellent. Our charity raises money solely by producing events, so we've seen many spaces, and worked with many event crews. Krystin had that perfect attitude we appreciate more than anything from day 1. She was constantly solution driven with a smile on her face the whole time. Not sure we had any requests that pushed the limits for her, but if so, it certainly never showed. That attitude seemed to flow throughout the rest of the staff as well.

Beyond that, the food was excellent and the bar service was great as well.

We hope to repeat the event again next year, and will look to The Ivory Room once again as long as you'll have us.

Thanks again to both of you, and please convey my compliments and thanks to the event staff as well.

All the best,

Rob Snow
Founder/Dad/Occasional Comic
Stand Up For Downs

recenca ~/30/18

Paul Trayser

March 26, 2018

Cameron Mitchell
Cameron Mitchell Restaurants
390 W Nationwide Blvd
Columbus, Ohio 43215

Dear Cameron:

As you may already know, I have recently stepped away from the wholesale wine distribution industry. It was a difficult decision, but it has allowed me to spend some time caring for my elderly parents.

I want to take this opportunity to thank you for the wonderful business relationship we've had over the past 25 years. Much of my career has been devoted to serving your company's adult beverage needs, and I want to let you know what an absolute pleasure it's been calling on your restaurants.

It has been an honor and a privilege to be associated with your company. Your managers and associates are the best in the business, and there is no question in my mind that I wouldn't have stayed as long as I did without these great relationships. It's been gratifying to watch many of them mature, learn, and be rewarded through advancement in the company.

It has also been fulfilling to watch the amazing growth of CMR, and I wish you the very best in your continued success.

Sincerely,

Paul Trayser

From: Doug Wolf
Sent: Wednesday, July 11, 2018 2:32 PM
To: Rebecca Asmo, Steve Weis
Subject: RE: Cameron Mitchell Workforce Partnership

Hi Steve,

Thanks again for connecting our young people to such meaningful work experiences. I'm looking forward to meeting with Lindsey at the conclusion of the summer to better understand Cameron Mitchell's approach to making Summer Youth Employment such a positive experience. Below are two stories that highlight the importance of our partnership and how this program reaches beyond simply having a "summer job."

- ███████ is a 16 year old girl who is now in her fifth week as a Summer Youth Employee at The Guild House. ███████ initially tasked with dishwashing, worked with her supervisor to develop new skills and relationships that allowed her to participate in allowable meal preparation work by the second week. Now she is working with The Guild House team to learn more about the food and supply ordering processes, systems and databases. She and her supervisor have established a goal to progress to shadowing more advanced roles within The Guild House while she continues to develop her specific work responsibilities. ███████ has consistently been treated as a valuable member of Cameron Mitchell team and has fallen in love with her job at The Guild House. The impact this experience has had on Rae'Niqua thus far is immeasurable, especially because this is her FIRST work experience.

- ███████ is also in his fifth week with Cameron Mitchell as a Summer Youth Employee at Rusty Bucket Arlington. ███████ is having an experience that equals that of ███████. In fact, I understand he is being considered for potential employment in the fall after the conclusion of the Summer Youth Employment program. Recently, ███████ had a heartwarming experience with an individual delivering supplies to the restaurant. ███████' father, who he had not seen in more than 3 months, was that individual delivering supplies. It seemed events lined up just so they would cross paths. We heard from the manager that it was a joyful encounter. ███████' father took great pride in seeing his son working and ███████ took great pride is seeing his father doing the same. This is a good reminder of the "ripple effect" of our work. We may never fully appreciate the depth and breadth of our impact but stories like this serve as great reminders and energizers.

It's clear that Cameron Mitchell Restaurant's takes seriously its commitment to its culture and community. We've witnessed this commitment throughout this summer. Our plan, as you know, calls for Access for All, Transformational Experiences and Best & Brightest Leaders. Cameron Mitchell Restaurants has, no doubt, helped us deliver upon those strategic priorities and, most importantly, deliver upon the commitment and promise we make to our young people every day.

Thanks for all that you do.

Doug Wolf, MS, MBA

Chief Strategy Officer

Boys & Girls Clubs of Columbus

1108 City Park Avenue, Suite 301

Columbus, OH 43206

www.bgccolumbus.org

From: Adam Merkel
Sent: Saturday, June 30, 2012 11:35 PM
To: Stacey Connaughton
Subject: Big Fan of Cameron Mitchell...PLEASE FORWARD

Hello Stacy, I am avid fan of Mr. Cameron Mitchell. It would mean the world to me if you could possibly forward this letter to him so he can have the opportunity to read it. Thank you very much!

Hello Mr. Mitchell, my name is Adam Merkel. First off this is not spam, I am a real person. You don't have a clue who I am, but I have been a HUGE fan of your restaurants for quite some time...which makes me a huge fan of yours!

Here's a little bit about me. I am 29 years old, married, with a beautiful wife and an amazing 1 1/2 year old little boy named Jack. I grew up in the restaurant business, and as a child I spent all of my free time watching and learning the business from my mother and my stepdad. My stepdad is Greek and had 3 family dining/coney islands pretty much my whole life so that was all I knew. Then to my surprise now 10 yr old brother was born and they decided to lease out all the buildings, step out of operations, and sell the businesses to semi-retire. At that time I was about 17, so I clearly wasn't ready or mature enough to own or operate a business. I jumped from job to job from kitchen to server in the corporate restaurant world trying to figure out my path. Then when I was 19 yrs old I fell into selling cars for Ford. Not knowing a thing about the business, someone gave me a chance and the rest was history. I quickly worked my way up and learned the ropes of the car business and earned a spot at the #1 ford dealer in the country Bill Brown Ford. I am proud to say I was the top salesperson for Ford in the U.S. in August of 09' selling and delivering 47 new vehicles that month.. In everything I've done in life I have always tried to learn something new every day, stay positive, and pick up habits of people who were the very best at what they do. That's why I am contacting you today.

I have had and will forever have a strong passion for food, the restaurant business, and most importantly people. About a year and a half ago, I decided to leave my 100k +/yr car sales job and partner with my mom and stepdad in a restaurant in downtown Howell, MI in hopes of someday owning and operating multiple places. It is called Diamond's Steaks & Seafood. The deal was to be on salary and to have a 33% cut of future profits but not including any true ownership, just of the profits, and not on paper. Some may call me crazy but when I walk into one of your restaurant concepts or any other place that in my opinion really GETS what people want, isn't afraid to try new things, and is extremely successful, I say to myself "I know I was born to do this". As you and I both know, a lot of people have "dreams" of owning their own restaurant and someday they might be able to fulfill that dream. However, very few are successful and have no idea how to run a business, manage people, and an even a smaller few can stand the test of time.

As I said before I only want to learn and pick up things from the very best, and when I walk into your restaurants I am truly inspired. I don't think it's just about having a great chef, or having the coolest new place, or just having great food. It's about giving everyday people what they really want, and at the end of the day being able to make money at it. My entire family owns businesses, whether it be a restaurant, a tree service, veterinarian, or you name it. I am willing to do whatever it takes to be successful and do anything and everything I can to do that. My goal is to be the next Cameron Mitchell and have multiple places that are all wildly successful.

Anyhow, I don't want to ramble on and take too much of you time because I know you have to be just an insanely busy guy. I know most people probably wouldn't send you this email who are in the business, but a lot of people already think they have all the answers. I am confident in my abilities, but I also believe the day you stop learning and the day you think you know it all is the day you should hang it up. So I'm not afraid to reach out to the people I believe do it best, and I know you are one of the *few* of those people. That's how I learned to sell cars the right way and that's how I believe you learn anything in life. We all know it's great to be lucky, but most of the time success has little to do with luck. It's about hard work, being persistent, staying true to yourself, making people feel that they are appreciated, and in my opinion putting your own ego aside and never being afraid of trying something different.

In a nutshell I would be so thrilled to get the opportunity to meet you and get any pointers you could give me about your story and what has and hasn't worked for you. I would love your feedback on that or anything else you would be so gracious to share with me. As I said, what you have accomplished and most of all where you came from really inspires me to work my butt off and realize that you really CAN achieve your goals through hard work, intense dedication, and most of all a true passion for hospitality. I have always tried to go confidently in the direction of my dreams, and live the life I've imagined and I would be beyond thrilled to be even half as successful as you have become.

I know that you are a growing company with philosophies and values I share not only as a restaurant guy but as a person. I believe that you have gotten to where you are today the right way, with integrity, and definitely not by chance. If at all possible in any way, shape, or form, I would love to be a part of that. Thank you again very much for even taking the time to read this and any help you could possibly give me would be immensely appreciated. It really does mean the world to me. Feel free to contact me anytime. Thanks a million!

Sincerely,

Adam Merkel

adam@merkelrestaurants.com

It is one of our customs to take a restaurant team photo prior to each restaurant's grand opening. These always warm my heart because the excitement and team feeling is so evident. Here are a couple of great examples of our associates ready to make Raving Fans:

Opening day at The Pearl, October 2012.

Opening day at Ocean Prime Naples, December 2016.

OUR PORTFOLIO OF BRANDS

CAMERON MITCHELL

· R E S T A U R A N T S ·

Great People Delivering Genuine Hospitality

MARTINI
modern italian

MITCHELL'S
OCEAN CLUB
SEAFOOD · STEAKS · COCKTAILS

The PEARL

CAMERON'S
American Bistro

OCEAN PRIME
SEAFOOD · STEAKS · COCKTAILS

HUDSON 29
KITCHEN + DRINK

CAMERON MITCHELL
PREMIER EVENTS

BUCKEYE HOSPITALITY

CONSTRUCTION LLC

Molly
Woo's

BUDD DAIRY CO
FOOD HALL

MARCELLA'S

THE BARN
A ROCKY FORK CREEK

THE GUILD HOUSE

THE
Avenue
— STEAK TAVERN —

HARVEY & ED'S

DEL MAR

M

CameronMitchell.com

INDEX